(1990)

THE FLOATING INFERNO

Patrick Stephens Limited, part of Thorsons, a division of the Collins Publishing Group, has published authoritative, quality books for enthusiasts for more than twenty years. During that time the company has established a reputation as one of the world's leading publishers of books on aviation, maritime, military, model-making, motor cycling, motoring, motor racing, railway and railway modelling subjects. Readers or authors with suggestions for books they would like to see published are invited to write to: The Editorial Director, Patrick Stephens Limited, Thorsons Publishing Group, Wellingborough, Northants, NN8 2RQ.

THE
FLOATING
INFERNO

The story of the loss of the Empress of Britain

ROBERT SEAMER

Patrick Stephens Limited

First published in 1990

British Library Cataloguing in Publication Data

Seamer, Robert
The floating inferno: the story of the loss of the
Empress of Britain.
I. Title
940.542

ISBN 1-85260-324-0

*Patrick Stephens Limited is part of the
Thorsons Publishing Group, Wellingborough,
Northamptonshire NN8 2RQ, England.*

Printed by Mackays of Chatham, Kent

1 3 5 7 9 10 8 6 4 2

'. . . and so in secret once again she slips
into the danger lanes of yesterday
to join her ruthless amorist, the sea.
Who woos her still with green and gold display
that on this final voyage must prevail
against both disregard and privilege . . .
So she goes down contemptuous of all
to some dim nave upon the ocean floor
Where faithful worshippers long dead
Conjoin to pledge the memory of one
Who formerly had ruled in dynasty . . .'

From *The Lost Liner* by Edmund Delorme,
Ship's Surgeon, *Empress of Britain*

To Nancy
The greatest blessing of my life

Contents

Acknowledgements

The author acknowledges with gratitude generously granted access to the following records and institutions, and the kindness of the many people listed below, who in our correspondence and conversations enthusiastically contributed to this true story of the sea.

Ministry of Defence, Archives, Hayes, Middlesex; Ministry of Defence, Naval Secretary's Office, London; Public Records Office, Kew (ADM.199/121–105, to 113); Mr George Bonwick, one-time Fifth Officer, *Empress of Britain*, Mercantile Consultant and author of several books on shipping; Captain G. Mansell, Retired Marine Superintendent and one-time Sixth Officer, *Empress of Britain*; Dr Edmund Delorme, MD, FRCS (Canada), retired London surgeon, one-time Ship's Surgeon, *Empress of Britain*; Commander Francis Warrington-Strong, DSC and Bar, RN (Ret'd); Canadian Pacific Company, London; Mr Bernard Jope, one-time Luftwaffe pilot and Commander and later Flight Captain, Lufthansa; The Earl of Yarborough, nephew of survivor; Mrs Rona Askew (was Mrs Trotter), survivor; Lady Joan Stephenson, survivor; Lady Wendy Lycett, daughter of survivor; Mr Colin Peck, one-time Editor of *Seanews*; Mrs Pat Spurgeon, wife of Senior Officer, rescuing ships; Mr H. Spurgeon, son of Senior Officer, rescuing ships; Mr F. Ellison, survivor; Mr John Trotter, son of survivor; Lufthansa, Berlin; Lieutenant-Commander H. Wolf, RN (Ret'd), ex-submarine Commander, who checked detail regarding submarines under attack.

The Authentic narrative is based on the following documents from the Public Records Office, Kew, Surrey, England: Report by Commander HMS *Broke* (ADM199/1887) (pp 271, 272); Report by Commander HM Tug *Seaman* (ADM199/1887) (pp 273); Report by Commander HMS *Harvester* (ADM199/121) (pp 105–108); Report by Commander HMS *Highlander* (ADM199/121) (pp 113); Proceedings and Findings of a Board of Enquiry held in Glasgow on 1 November 1940 (ADM/1/11180-NL 13729/1940).

Introduction

Between 0920 and 0950 on 26 October 1940 the fabulously luxurious Canadian Pacific liner *Empress of Britain* was devastated by fire after a number of bombs struck her. In the next few hours she struggled for survival and, but for the misfortunes of war and possibly some misjudgements on the part of those sent to help her, she might have made it safely back to port. She was badly hurt, gutted utterly by overwhelming fire and incapable of self-movement. But the next day, assisted by two tugs and guarded by two destroyers, she was on her way back home. She could have been hospitalized and nursed and in time gone back to sea, not as the epitome of peacetime luxury for which she was famous the whole world over, but as a huge ship which could have played a most important part in the transportation of troops, food and war materials to any place in the world and, which made her unique, by any route.

She was a most important vessel and very badly needed at a time when Britain could within weeks have been starved into submission by the failure of her merchant fleet. There were 42,348 tons of her, her size and capacity planned so that she could pass through the Panama and Suez canals. No other merchant ship of her tonnage could make such a passage.

At a Board of Enquiry held some days later it was found that after the bombing attack the *Empress* had spontaneously blown up under the impact of exploding ammunition in her magazine or exploding gases in her oil tanks formed by the heat of the fires which gutted her. The Board of Enquiry had not been told about the U-boat *U32*.

The *Empress* did not blow up. She was *blown* up by at least one of a number of torpedoes fired at her by *U32*. In the early hours of 28 October, whilst the *Empress* was under tow and proceeding at an inviting 4 knots, the U-boat found her and, after some manoeuvring, crept through the destroyer screen, attacked and dispatched her. And such are the oddities of war that two days later on the 30 October, *U32* was trapped by two Royal Navy warships, HMS *Harvester* and HMS *Highlander* and was herself dispatched.

But that is the aftermath of the *Empress of Britain* story, and at that time no one knew of the role played by *U32* in her destruction. The full story is told in the latter part of this book.

The *Empress* was not only of great importance in wartime, but in peacetime had been incomparably beyond her rivals in most aspects of *worldwide* travel. She was the largest ship ever to travel between all Commonwealth ports, and the largest and most luxurious ever to travel that most profitable route, the St Lawrence. She was the first really big ship ever built especially for luxury world touring and beyond doubt could give more luxury and comfort to her passengers, *anywhere in the world*, than any other ship before or after.

She was not the world's largest ship, not by a long chalk. Even the old four-funneller *Aquitania* was bigger. So had been the tragic *Titanic* of 1912, and so were, of course, those fabulous ships of the late 'thirties, *Queen Mary* and *Normandie*, but these great ships were built primarily for the North Atlantic and could not pass through the great canals. Finally, in the realm of truly great ships, as far as innovation and speed were concerned came the greatest of them all, the magnificent but hopelessly too-late United States Line pride, *United States*, which so easily wrested the mystic Blue Riband from the 'Mary'. But this was post-war, at a time when the airlines were taking over the Atlantic crossing and ships' speed, comfort and capacity in the handling of transatlantic travel had, regrettably, become irrelevant.

The once-a-year arrival of the fabulous *Empress* in any of the far-flung ports she visited, from Quebec of the chilly breezes to Singapore and its steamy heat, from the blasts of 'windy' Wellington to the lethargy of Tahiti, was an event. She was a sight whose arrival drew the city dwellers of every port to see and admire, not to be missed at any price by ship-lovers who, although they would never have the good fortune to sail in her, nevertheless would not miss the next best thing—an outing with the family just to see her sailing into their port with her magnificent nose stuck majestically in the air and, perhaps, if the authorities were kind, a conducted tour of her. We are speaking now, of course, of the well-blessed times before terrorism became a normal daily hazard. It is rare indeed, nowadays, that the public are invited to inspect a ship in port.

She was the Great White Ship which even during the depression years of the 'thirties anomalously plied her way through the wide waters of a world beyond the world, loaded but never over-loaded with assorted millionaires, the wealthy of all nations, people whose names were a byword, sportsmen, film stars, prime ministers and, even beyond these, the highest of all the mortal highs—King George V and his charming Queen Mary—followed, as the crises of the 'thirties neared their breaking points, by King George VI and, still beloved today as the Queen Mother, Queen Elizabeth. The British Empire had not yet tumbled over the precipice although she was hovering near the edge, and who could have been greater figures of goodness and duty in that uncertain world than those most beloved of all the monarchs of the great House of Windsor?

So much can be said about the *Empress*—that she had swimming pools, turkish baths and massage rooms, that there were cinemas, concert halls, gymnasiums, squash courts, a full-sized tennis court; that there were hairdressing salons and beauty parlours to gild the world's wealthiest lilies and the most fully equipped hospital ever to embellish a passenger ship, supplemented by an ultra-modern dental surgery. A passage on the *Empress* was the culminating peak of all things that money could buy, and looking at it through the eyes of P. G. Wodehouse's Monty Bodkin, all it lacked were a few hundred acres of rough shooting.

At that time this capacity and spaciousness at sea were luxuries beyond dreams, outrageously improving upon the already luxurious *Duchess of York* which, at a mere 22,000 gross tons and catering for 1,559 passengers, was the Queen of that part of the Canadian Pacific fleet which plied the Atlantic Ocean.* Not only did the *Empress* practically double the

---

* The Canadian Pacific liner *Empress of Japan* had a gross tonnage of 26,300 tons, but she plied the Pacific Ocean and not, until wartime, the Atlantic.

13

Duchess's tonnage but she also catered for 430 *fewer* passengers. The space and elegance may be imagined.

An article published in America after her destruction said: 'The world cruises of the ill-fated ship were known to most people. However, only those richly endowed and possessed of abundant leisure could enjoy them.' However true this was—and such anomalies have always been with us and are still with us in these days of the allegedly great, bland levelling—what of it? The author noted that for one survivor who had been a young soldier in Singapore in 1938 earning possibly four shillings a day, there was no resentment of this demonstration of great wealth as the *Empress* came flaunting it into Singapore harbour. Rather, he said, he would just have liked to be one of the lucky ones who could enjoy her.

During her last Atlantic voyage before the war she carried King George VI and Queen Elizabeth from Conception Bay, Newfoundland, to Southampton. It was the last of her truly luxurious trips and one crew member was to enjoy a special luxury he had not bargained for. He was appointed to attend the Royal party and one day the King asked him if he could repair his movie camera. As he was working in the luxury suite, the Queen came in and gave him a cigar. He put it in his pocket. So the Queen gave him another, which he was to smoke. Enter the King. He sniffed. 'Ah!' he said, 'I see you smoke the same cigars as I do!'

There are many stories of the *Empress* whilst she was living but this book is about the way she was to die. Fifty years later most of the people involved in her death have passed on. But some are still with us. To get at the true story it was necessary first to examine the statements made by the 27 witnesses at the Board of Enquiry. Next, to search for still living survivors. Then to begin a detailed correspondence with people who had taken some part in the action, to visit some of them and to do a lot of reading at relevant institutions, which also involved some considerable correspondence.

Some of the evidence was contradictory, some of it confusing and some overlapping. Some was incorrect, some inexplicit and, today, impossible to clarify. One of the difficulties was that people told the same story from different points of view, so there was bound to be some distorted repetition—and, of course, disagreement. Further, in the horror of that tragic day, very few of those involved had much idea of what the time

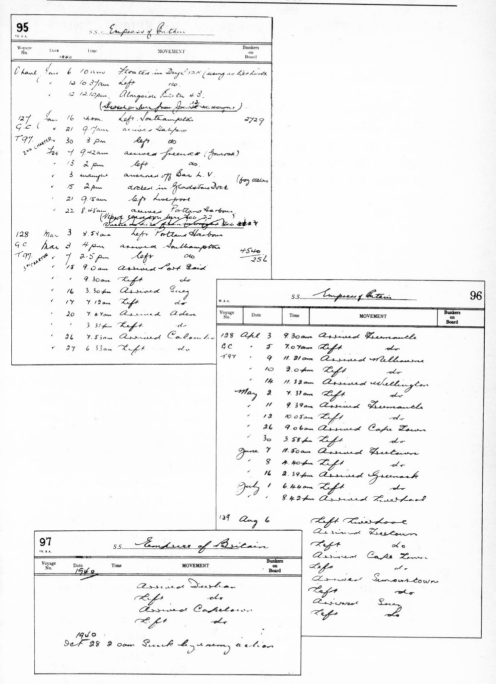

The last three pages of the Empress of Britain's *log, which appears to be in Capt Sapsworth's handwriting. (PRO, Kew, and Controller of HM Stationery Office; ADM 121, pp95-7)*

was or of what was happening in parts of the ship where they were not.

*   *   *

On 2 September 1939, the day before the Second World War was declared by Great Britain, the *Empress* sailed from Southampton with her largest ever complement of passengers. People were dodging the war to come, and children were being rushed to safety. She arrived in Quebec on 8 September. They painted her grey and sailed her to Halifax, Nova Scotia, where she was laid up. She was requisitioned as a troopship on 25 November and on 10 December she sailed for the Clyde, where she arrived on 17 December. On 7 March 1940 she went via Suez, Aden, Colombo and Melbourne to Wellington where she arrived on 14 April. She joined what was to be known as the 'Million Dollar Convoy', routed originally via Suez and the Mediterranean. But now Italy had entered the war and had forces along the Red Sea, in Eritrea, Italian Somaliland and North Africa as well as in Italy itself, so the *Empress* was re-routed via the Cape and Freetown, Sierra Leone. She arrived in Liverpool on 1 June. She left on 6 August bound for Suez via the Cape. She was never to visit her homeland again, although she got so very, very near.

On 23 September she left Suez. She called at Durban and Cape Town. Because of her speed she sailed from the Cape unescorted with an estimated date of arrival in Liverpool of 28 October. But on the 26th, about 60 miles off the north-west Irish coast, she was attacked by a German aircraft and set on fire.

1

Saturday, 26 October 1940: the attack

Forenoon: North-east Atlantic

On 26 October 1940 Commander Stanley Henlein King Spurgeon, DSO Royal Australian Navy, was commander of HMS *Echo*. *Echo* was one of four warships escorting two troopships, HMT *Ettrick* and HMT *Kranga* from Gibraltar to the Clyde, where they were due to arrive on 28 October.

An escort of four warships for two troopers seems incredible when one thinks of the lack of escorts for ships returning to the UK from the Middle East at this time, *Empress of Britain*, *Strathaird*, *Strathnaver*, *Franconia* and *Andes* being among them. However, rumour had it that the two troopships were the remnants of an aborted attack on Dakkar in what was then French Senegal, in which case a strong escort would be understandable.

The other ships of the escort were HMS *Escapade*, HMS *Burza* and HMS *Blyskawica*, the latter two being ships of the Polish Navy which had escaped, when Europe fell to the Germans, to join the British Navy.

Commander Spurgeon's second-in-command in *Echo* was Lieutenant Terrence Tibbits, First Lieutenant or, in naval parlance, 'Jimmy the One'. The next most senior officer was Lieutenant Francis Warrington-Strong, known to his friends then and now as 'Warry'. He was the ship's navigating officer.

These two officers, although young, were fully trained and experienced and were the only seaman branch officers holding

17

watchkeeping certificates apart, of course, from Commander Spurgeon. They were working what was known as 'watch-and-watch', being four hours on the bridge followed by four hours off duty, this latter including eating and sleeping times. Frequently the off-duty watchkeeper was called out from whatever rest he was snatching and it was not unusual for him to spend 12 hours or even more on duty. Much of the time these officers were cold, tired, wet and hungry and they were always short of sleep. Any officer who was on a small Royal Navy ship during the harsh winter of 1940–41 in the North Atlantic will tell the same story. A tough, anxious and unpleasant time was had by all.

Commander Spurgeon carried a load even heavier than his juniors, for his was the overall responsibility. He was, in effect, 'watch-on-stop-on', liable to be called out from his sea cabin under the bridge whenever someone or something was thought to require his attention. In other words, no matter where he was or what he was doing, he was still on duty. There was no time off.

The affair of the *Empress of Britain* began for these officers early in the forenoon of the 26 October when a distress message from her was intercepted. The signal gave her position and stated that she was being heavily bombed. Half an hour later a further signal was picked up saying that her crew was taking to the boats and the ship was being abandoned.

At 1030 the Commanding Officer of *Escapade*, who was senior officer of the convoy, received a message from Flag Officer in Charge, Greenock, ordering him to detach two destroyers to go and investigate the bombing. *Escapade* detailed *Echo* and *Burza*, and they were ordered to proceed forthwith.

At this time the two ships were about 100 miles south-west of the *Empress* and would have had a total of nearly 500 miles to steam to make the Clyde if they diverted to her. But as it happened, all the destroyers of the escort were down to about 30 per cent of their fuel oil, and under adverse circumstances there was some doubt whether they could make the journey at an uneconomical high speed and still reach the Clyde without refuelling.

Signals were exchanged on this matter. The result was that within 15 minutes of the message from Greenock being received by *Escapade*, *Echo* and *Burza* had detached and, oil or no oil, were on their way at top speed for the *Empress of*

Britain lying at position 55.08 north by 10.46 west, about 60 miles off the north-west Irish coast.

What had happened to the famous *Empress*? And what was still to happen? And what was so important about her that at a time when the Germans were sinking Allied ships with monotonous regularity (already more than 410 ships, representing 1,158,190 tons, had been destroyed), the successful attack upon her had been reported immediately to the German Supreme Headquarters and they had gone so far as to send out a reconnaissance plane to check on the report?

0400: Base Bordeaux-Merignac, occupied France

It began at 0400 at the German airbase at Bordeaux–Merignac in occupied France, when Oberleutnant Bernard Jope (pronounced 'Yopper'), commanding a Focke-Wulf C200 Condor, set off on an armed weather reconnaissance flight over the Atlantic west of Ireland. The crew consisted of one flight officer, one mechanic, two radio operators, one air gunner, one meteorologist, and the commander. The crew had been well rested and were looking forward to their flight.

The fully loaded FW C200 was an awkward plane to get off the ground, being simply a pre-war Lufthansa passenger Condor adapted as a long-range fighting plane. The passenger part had been filled with rubber-protected fuel containers and provided a working place for the mechanic. In the bow, under and behind the cockpit and slightly off-set to the right, a ventral gondola had been installed with a 2cm cannon. Similarly, a blister had been added on top of the fuselage behind the cockpit. The plane did not normally seek fights with other aircraft because its armour was weak and its steering was too slow and unresponsive. In flight it was heavily overloaded with its full racks of 250kg (550-lb) high explosive bombs and enough fuel for a 15-hour flight. Stationary on the runway the fuselage had to be supported, and in taking off fully loaded there was always the danger that it would 'break out' (the expression is Oberleutnant Bernard Jope's). There had been several losses that way. Its speed was 270–300 km per hour, at most 180 miles per hour.

In spite of these weaknesses, the plane was to cause many problems for the embattled British merchant fleet, sinking many ships, damaging others, acting as 'spotters' for U-boats and coming to be referred to by Winston Churchill as 'the scourge of the Atlantic'.

On this day the weather was bad for flying. Low clouds reduced visibility and, being early winter, there was only feeble light in the early morning. Because of the low rain cloud Jope flew his plane low. They came across the *Empress* by luck and not, as some media reported, because Jope had intercepted a wireless message.

0730: *Empress of Britain*

Captain C. H. Sapsworth, CVO, Master of the *Empress of Britain* was out of his bed by 0730. His bedroom steward had awoken him with his early morning tea-tray. He swung his legs over and touched the carpet, and then went into the bathroom between his bedroom and dining room. He returned, poured himself a cup of tea and wandered over to look out of the window over the captain's bridge in front of his suite and beyond to the forecastle.

Sapsworth was a small man, wizened, narrow in the shoulder. He never seemed quite big enough to fill out his uniform properly and sometimes he wished he were bigger. When he thought like that he had formed the habit of hardening his mind, throwing out his chest and raising his chin. He might not be very big but he had a lot to be proud of.

Like a true sailor he had, as he often reminded himself, gone through the salt-sea mill. He had served before the mast under sail. He had entered the employ of Canadian Pacific on 15 March 1912, 28 years before. He held an Extra Masters' Certificate. One of his junior officers described him as an effeminate type, shy and remote; he had a charming way with the ladies. Obviously that particular officer did not get along with his Captain and indeed, as he admitted, rarely saw him. One suspects that the officer had a slight penchant to the left and was mildly resentful of an elite authority.

But another of the ship's officers described Captain Sapsworth as a dedicated and able seaman of whom he was very fond. But even he admitted that Sapsworth had none of the larger-than-life charisma of some of the captains of the great passenger liners. Still, he had been master of the *Empress* when George VI crossed the Atlantic aboard her with his Queen, and not every ship's master would have been deemed suitable for such an honour.

The trouble with Captain Sapsworth was that he was shy—that most heartbreaking of all afflictions to those who suffer from it, and at the same time that reason for contempt and intolerance on the part of those who do not and who cannot understand it. Even so, the author is told, Captain Sapsworth was a consummate seaman. Indeed, he must have been to achieve the elevation he had. For example—as Dr Eddy Delorme, the ship's surgeon, affirms—Sapsworth had for the first time in the ship's history missed going aground on the sandbar at the entrance to the Bitter Lakes halfway along the Suez Canal when he insisted on taking over from the official pilot.

Another of his minor achievements as a master of large vessels—and again, the author is indebted to Dr Delorme for this information—was that he brought the *Empress* into 'Windy' Wellington in New Zealand and placed her directly alongside the pier at a time when, because of the weather, the port pilot said it could not be done.

Whilst ships' masters and pilots today would not recommend this sort of independence—in 1984 the Commander of a Royal Navy frigate refused the assistance and ignored the advice of an experienced pilot in the Thames and said goodbye to his pension as he crashed his ship into Tower Bridge—perhaps back in the war days masters necessarily had more freedom. One ship's master, Captain of a 22,000-ton cruise ship within recent years, told the author that nowadays he was so tied to his head office in London and local port bureaucracies that he felt like nothing more than a post office.

Sapsworth glanced at his barometer, thought little of it and stared out of the window at the gently trembling, rising and falling stem 160 feet in front of him, feeling the satisfaction and almost aesthetic pleasure of a true seaman as he watched it shiver at the apex of its rise before slowly descending. The horizon was a light grey line dividing the dark grey sky from the equally dark grey of the comfortably active sea. The stem repeatedly broke this dividing line as it rose and fell.

The bedroom steward had turned on the fresh hot water bath and the steam coming through the door was an invitation. Sapsworth manipulated the 'Shanks' taps and stepped into the tub, eyes still sleepy, and settled with a grunt of pleasure into the soft, warm water. Like everyone else he was experiencing that mild thrill of excitement that stirs wanderers by sea as they approach a home port. He had been away for nearly three months and was now approaching the United Kingdom, having come up eastwards of the Azores to a position 50 degrees north and 23 degrees west prior to making a cautious approach to his present position about 60 miles from the north-west Irish coast.

The Naval Control Service Officer at Cape Town had given him complete discretion as to speed in order to make his oil last all the way to Liverpool, and had also given him the option of calling at Freetown if necessary. But working it out they found that he could make the journey at an average speed of 20 knots without refuelling. Sapsworth decided to make a speed of 18 knots to the Equator and 22 knots from there to Liverpool, thus giving him the extra speed in the area of greatest danger. It would still leave him a couple of knots up his sleeve if it were necessary to proceed at full speed.

They had discussed the probable date of arrival at Liverpool and found that the average of 20 knots would get the ship there on Sunday 27 October, but owing to winter time and possible heavy weather it was decided to make it early on Monday 28th. NCSO Cape Town said he would cable the Admiralty to that effect. But owing to favourable currents south of the Equator and unusually fine weather north of it, they were well ahead of their ETA and it was decided to carry on at the same speed, 22 knots and try to make the Bar Light in time for Sunday morning's tide. And it is upon such fortuitous circumstances as this that the world goes on from crisis to crisis, and apparently unremarkable circumstances become momentous.

Sapsworth had a short talk on the telephone with Mr Stanley Keay, First Officer, who was relieving the senior officer of the watch. Mr Keay confirmed that they were doing a steady 22 knots, that there was a slight easterly wind which would freshen during the day, and a moderate swell. They were making their zig-zags in accordance with the set pattern and all was well.

But there were qualms of apprehension too, as anyone who travelled those dangerous waters regularly at that time will recall. So far Captain Sapsworth had not encountered direct action in the war, but he knew that a powerful and daring enemy, who probably knew exactly where he was, could be waiting for him. This disquieting uncertainty and fear was shared by everyone on board. They slept in their clothes with their lifejackets at hand. That tension was also shared by those who lurked beneath the surface.

However, here they were within a few miles of the Irish coast and entering the North West Approaches with the hope, but not the promise, of an RAF escort. There was also the comforting thought that they could outrun the fastest submarine with ease and that they were due in Liverpool tomorrow morning, beating their original estimated date of arrival by 24 hours.

Sapsworth hurried through his breakfast. He wished he did not feel so edgy. Was it possible that his unease, more than a general awareness of danger, was a premonition that within a couple of hours this magnificent ship would be a blazing, devastated and untenable inferno; that within 10 hours it would be a gutted hull, devoid of every aspect of life and luxury? That he would be a captain who had lost his ship? And that within a further 35 hours the *Empress of Britain* would heel over on her port side, give a last heartbreaking shudder as the sea engulfed her and disappear forever into the historic wreck-haunted waters of the North East Atlantic?

Those who believe in this sort of thing may think so. Sapsworth was a Scot, and a lonely and sensitive man as are all shy people; remote and susceptible as he was, he may also have been fey. As will be seen, he was not the only one who, more than being aware of danger, anticipated it.

By 0900 Captain Sapsworth was in the chartroom abaft the wheelhouse immediately above his personal suite and one level down from the compass platform. Surface visibility was full and he could see the grey horizon plainly. Above it things were not so good. The clouds were between seven and eight tenths with a ceiling of about 3,000 feet. There were some low rain clouds meandering below half-overcast stratus. The conditions were perfect for a surprise air attack, for a plane could hide above the low cloud and approach clandestinely.

The guns had been manned since dawn. The 6-inch naval gun and the 3-inch high-angle gun on the after deck were closed up for cleaning whilst the light automatics, First World War vintage Lewis guns, were also manned on the wings of the navigating bridge and amidships on each side abreast of the second funnel. Anti-aircraft lookouts were posted on the upper bridge, port and starboard, and on the docking bridge aft near the 6-inch and 3-inch guns.

Under good conditions it was quite possible to hear easily the noise of a plane from the bridge even up to a distance of perhaps five miles, although wind and storm naturally affected this. But on this occasion Oberleutnant Jope's Condor was to leeward and the wind would have carried its noise away. With the low ceiling, therefore, it is quite understandable that no one knew the plane was there until it was quite close.

0920: 'It's a Jerry, Chief!'

Jope was flying west. The *Empress* was steaming east. The meteorologist was first to see her. What he saw was a large ship with three funnels on the port side of his plane. He informed his commander that they were approaching 'a large pot'. Jope made a slight turn to starboard to give him a better view and a wider arc to turn in. Then he swung round to port to approach the ship from due astern.

In the cloudy weather and poor light there was always the possibility of losing sight of the quarry, so Jope pushed his plane down to about 100 metres. This was the first attack. Later he was to come in at little more than mast height.

His gunner opened fire with his cannon from the under fuselage gondola and at the same time a huge bomb was released and, bearing in mind that this was the youthful, 26-year-old Jope's first operational flight, he had all the traditional good luck of the beginner, hitting the *Empress* amidships. And what a hit it turned out to be.

As the Condor opened fire, the guns on the *Empress* returned it and they too scored significant hits on the plane, damaging her bombsight to an extent that it could not effectively be used again. The Condor flew ahead and veered off to starboard, turning to circle the ship. It then repeated its attack once more from astern. This time the bombs missed—and there is a photograph taken by the meteorologist to prove it.

For reasons which Jope does not explain, but probably because by this time the ship was already smothered in a thick pall of yellowy-black smoke which obscured the after part (and again there is a photograph to prove it), spoiling what had hitherto been a lovely target, Jope went forward well past the bows and then returned to attack from ahead. He severely machine-gunned the bridge and indeed the whole length of the ship, although he could not now see it all. He also dropped his last bombs. The open promenade deck abaft the third funnel above the isolation hospital was badly hit and the 3-inch HA gun on the docking bridge was put out of action. The boat deck was blazing, as were the sports deck and tennis court. Amidships there was a huge conflagration on the lounge deck. Adding to the holocaust many lifeboats and rafts had been destroyed and others set on fire.

At about this time the plane received more hits and one of her engines began losing oil. Jope switched it off, cut his mission short and headed for home, although the damaged engine meant that he did not make it all the way in one go. He landed at Brest, had his engine repaired and flew next day to Bordeaux–Merignac where he was greeted with uninhibited delight. Let us quote Bernard Jope, writing to the author 43 years later:

'After the attack my radio operator reported success to our base. We did not know immediately what vessel we had hit and our assessment of the size of the ship was completely wrong. I reported as follows: "General location fair sized trading vessel, approximately 20,000 tons attacked successfully, there will be losses, listing, the boats are down". Only after our touchdown in Brest did we learn the facts. The reception next day at Base Merignac by the Commandant, First Lieutenant Petersen, was wildly enthusiastic.'

And after all it was not a bad effort on a young commander's first operational flight, to destroy what had been one of the world's most important merchant ships in a matter of half an hour, good luck notwithstanding. Good luck is a pool we all dip into with the clearest of conscience and the greatest of glee.

A telex sent from Jope's unit to German Supreme Headquarters was intercepted by British intelligence. It translates:

> Command Section   26th October,
> Group Ic.   20.45.
>
> KR Telex to Gr. IMS Kurfurst, Robinson Ic
> Caesar Ic[1], M. Gr. Kdo. West[2], Lfl. 5[3] over Ob. d.L.[4] and
> W-Leit 3[5] over L. V. Paris[6].
>
> ---
>
> Individual Report No. 5 of 26.10.40.
> *Successful sinkings*: Air Corps IV.
> 1 FW 200 of I. K.G. 40 Start 0409 h.
> Attack 10.30 on s.s. *Empress of Britain* (42,000t) in square
> 1676/25 West (140 km west of isles of Aran), course east
> with 6 SC 250. 2 SC 250 in target. Fire on board, ship
> listing. Destruction to be expected. Ship sent SOS after
> bombing and radioed that crew were taking to boats.
> There was light flak and M.G. defence from the ship
> which caused several hits to the plane. The commander
> of the crew was flying officer Jope.

[1] Codes of the German Supreme headquarters
[2] Marine-Group Commando West
[3] Airfleet 5
[4] Chief Commanding Officer of the Air Force.
[5] An Armed Forces Liaison Office
[6] Probably a radio operating post in Paris

The report was considered at Supreme Headquarters to be so
important that a reconnaissance plane—another Condor—was
sent out immediately to check on it. This was no ordinary
sinking.

* * *

Chief Petty Officer Jevans was a retired regular Navy man
who, like so many other retired servicemen bored with 'Civvy
Street', had welcomed the opportunity to get back to sea at the
outbreak of war. His appointment to the DEMS (Defensively
Equipped Merchant Ships) had been welcomed, especially as
his posting had been to the luxurious *Empress* rather than to
one of Walter de la Mare's 'dirty British coasters' such as had
fallen to the lot of less fortunate men in his situation. Jevans
was in charge of the ship's permanent gunners and also of
those men serving temporarily as light anti-aircraft gunners

detailed for the duty from military and naval personnel in transit.

He had issued orders to his men on the first half of the forenoon watch—0800 to 1000—to close up for cleaning and ammunition shifting. The after guns in his charge were the 3-inch high-angle gun (anti-aircraft) on the docking bridge and the 6-inch naval gun abaft and below it at the extreme after part of the open promenade deck. Among the men on duty were Able-Bodied Seamen Henry Petch, Ronald Pullen, Arthur Hipwell, John Webb and another named Andrews whose first name is not known. Except for the old hand, CPO Jevans, Petch was the only man with previous experience in action. He had served with HMS *Hostile* in the Skagerrak against German MTBs.

At 0915 Petch and Pullen were cleaning the 3-inch gun. Hipwell and Webb were lookouts, Hipwell to starboard, Webb to port, keeping their eyes skinned for anything unusual such as an aircraft, surface craft or the wake of a periscope. Upon sighting anything suspicious their duty was to shout to the gun crew who would man the appropriate gun, the 6-inch for a periscope or surface craft, the 3-inch for an aircraft. All ratings were fully trained on both guns.

AB Andrews was on telephone duty at the after steering position below and before the docking bridge. His job was to take and pass on to Jevans any messages from the navigating bridge or to notify the officer of the watch of anything untoward brought to his attention.

It may have been Petch's experience and an extra wary eye which made him the first to spot the approaching plane. It was a little before 0920. He pointed it out to his mates. It was on the port quarter, he thought between 3,000 and 4,000 yards away, at an angle of sight of 5 degrees. Hipwell immediately reported it to CPO Jevans, who also observed it. It was still a fair distance away—visibility was not good and he did not identify it as an enemy. It is possible that he was negligent in not instructing Andrews immediately to notify the bridge. It is also possible that since he received no warning from the bridge, either by docking telegraph or telephone, he assumed the plane to be a Coastal Command patrol. After all, there had been rumours—not emanating from a not very sanguine bridge, let it be said—that there would be an RAF escort through these dangerous waters; one sometimes wonders where such optimistic rumours arise, suspecting that they may be the offspring of fear and hope rather than experience and promise. Jevans did, however, issue an order to close up for action, and all continued to observe. In any case, the men were already at their guns and were aware of the approaching aircraft.

Petch thought it was at an altitude of about 1,000 feet and then at an angle of sight of 4 degrees when he saw, or thought he saw, a flash of light from its cabin, and this at first made him think the plane was friendly. But when it turned directly towards the stern he quickly changed his mind and shouted to Jevans. The four engines were now clearly visible and told their tale, for at that stage of the war Britain had no four-engined fighting aircraft.

'It's a Jerry, Chief!'

Petch then saw, or again thought he saw, the plane drop two Very lights, both of them red. Suddenly a bomb was seen to leave the plane and action erupted with bursts of cannon fire. Webb opened fire with the 3-inch and Petch beside him watched the bomb coming down. It struck amidships. Immediately a massive eruption of thick smoke rose from forward of the tennis court. Caught in the draught of the ship's passage the cloud quickly engulfed the entire upper structure abaft the centre funnel and with a south-easterly wind on the starboard beam the entire port side quickly disappeared under an ever-thickening pall.

Webb was still firing when the bomb hit the deck. Later he was to say that there were two bombs. It had also seemed to him as he swung the gun round to keep his target in sight that the aircraft had lifted its nose as though it were surprised by the return fire. He noted too that the guns on the bridge and abreast of the centre funnel were firing and that almost immediately there was a surge in the ship's movement as she heeled over to swing to port at high speed.

★ ★ ★

Petty Officer George Adlam was port side lookout on the upper bridge. He had been on duty since 0800 on a two-hour watch. Shortly before 0920 he saw with some surprise and relief a plane coming out of the clouds on the port beam flying an almost parallel but opposite course. It was at an angle of sight of about 30 degrees and about a quarter of a mile away. The surprise was because it was so close—the relief because he supposed it to be the rumoured escort. But still he did not identify it and in the normal course of duty he reported it to the relieving officer of the watch, First Officer Stanley Keay. At the same time he called to PO Cluett who was starboard lookout. The signalman of the watch, PO Tewry, had also seen the plane and he had reported it to Mr William Howell, relieving junior officer of the watch. Howell and the First Officer briefly discussed it and Keay told Howell to sound the air raid alarm. The gunners on the navigating bridge wings closed up on their guns.

The three ratings Adlam, Cluett and Tewry watched the aircraft circle towards the stern, saw it pass out of sight behind the funnels and then reappear briefly sharp on the starboard quarter coming towards the stern. It must be remembered that the observers on the bridge were getting a different view of things from those at the after part of the ship, although it seems that the latter may have seen the plane before those forward, because Adlam reported it as being only a quarter of a mile away compared to the 3–4,000 yards estimated by Petch. It may be that the lookouts on the upper bridge completely misjudged the distance. If indeed it was only a quarter of a mile away, why was it not identified? The Captain himself said in his evidence at the Board of Enquiry that '. . . all we could make out was that it was a four-engined monoplane . . .', and if he knew that, then he should also have known that it was an enemy. It all appears to have been a little casual.

Cluett saw the plane drop two Very lights, one, he thought, was green and the other red. Petch on the docking bridge thought they were both red. Both Cluett and Petch supposed these lights to be known signals for the bridge and assumed the aircraft to be friendly. Also on the upper bridge was Leading Signalman Sydney Newstead, leading signalman of the watch. He too saw the Very lights but thought that they were a green and a white or else two green.

Their assumption that the new arrival was their escort coming along to see them safely home was rudely shattered when they heard cannon shells crashing their dotted lines of holes and splinters along the sports deck. The gunners on the navigating bridge immediately returned the fire. Cluett, Adlam, Newstead and Tewry on the upper bridge were not manning guns so they dived down a ladder for cover, entered the wheelhouse and fell prone; or rather, Adlam and Cluett did. Newstead and Tewry, once at the bottom of the ladder, stood on the wing of the navigating bridge to watch. They heard the huge explosion and saw the immediate eruption of smoke from amidships, just abaft the centre funnel.

* * *

Mr Howell was Fourth Officer and was at this time relieving Mr Mansell, Sixth Officer, as junior officer of the watch. Mansell was at breakfast.

When PO Tewry reported the sighting of a plane on the port side, Howell went over to the bridge wing to observe it. He could see no markings and in the poor light he was unable to identify it. He reported it to the First Officer, Mr Keay, who as we know had already been informed. He could not identify the plane either, and ordered Howell to sound the air raid alarm. He then went to the chartroom and reported to Captain Sapsworth. The Captain noted the plane's slight swing away to its starboard and this made him think that it was friendly because escorting planes usually kept their distance and circled outside bombing range to avoid dangerous mistakes. In any event he was not prepared for the swing to port which brought the attacking plane across the ship's line of passage and on to her stern.

The sudden burst of cannon fire and machine-gun fire and the sight of the bomb leaving the plane momentarily froze him. He issued no orders to the guns and neither was the docking telegraph used to warn those aft. In any case, the gunners themselves did not wait to be told what to do when they were under cannon fire, and they opened up. It was just as well they did, for it was the Lewis gunners' first bursts which destroyed the plane's bombsight.

Straightening up immediately after the bomb explosion, the Captain dived back into the chartroom to see what had happened abaft the bridge. He passed Mr Howell in the wheelhouse, who had gone to sound the alarm. In the event he was pre-empted by one of the quartermasters who had sounded it without being told. Abaft the bridge the horrified Captain saw the thick smoke belch upwards where, caught by the wind, down it came again onto the decks cutting out all visibility between the bridge and after parts of the ship. He did not know at that stage that that first bomb (or bombs, for the question of accompanying incendiaries arose), after striking the sun deck, had pierced it, penetrated into the lounge deck and erupted with massive violence in the Mayfair Lounge with such cataclysmic force that an instantaneous, all-consuming fire filled the place from deck to dome, choking the nearby alleyways and vestibules with yellow and black smoke. It was an inferno.

Taking over command from the First Officer, Sapsworth almost instinctively rang down full speed on the telegraph and directed the shocked quartermaster to steer hard to port so that the after gun, the 3-inch, could keep the plane in its sights, being now off the starboard bow.

The Captain could hear the klaxons grating, notifying the alert, and he assumed that they could be heard throughout the ship. He did not know that the first attack had destroyed much of the ship's electrical and communications equipment, among other things. And among those other things, tragically, were the ship's fire-fighting capability and many of the boats. His assumption therefore that everyone with a duty to do would set about doing it without further instruction, and that those without specific duties would abide by air raid alarm drills, that is go below and lie on the deck, was not valid, for in many parts of the ship the alarm could not be heard. And although he could see the heavy pall of smoke over the centre of the ship, he did not yet know about the holocaust below, with most passageways between fore and aft impassable.

But his guns were still firing and he hoped that they would keep the plane away. It was a pretty desperate hope for as anyone who, in the days before computerized and radio-directed missiles, faced air attack on board ship with only minor armament will know, to hit a plane in full flight one has to be lucky. One is not far from being a sitting duck.

The guns continued to fire throughout the attacks which followed until, approximately half an hour later, the 3-inch gun received an almost direct bomb hit. By this time the burning ship was untenable.

* * *

Captain Bertram Nicholson RN was on his way home to a posting in the United Kingdom. At Port Suez he had been appointed Commodore of the convoy which included *Empress of Britain*, *Strathaird*, *Andes* and *Franconia*. Originally it had been supposed that the convoy would retain its composition all the way to Liverpool and would pick up an escort at Cape Town, and rumour had it that the escort would include that elusive aircraft carrier *Ark Royal*. But as always seemed to happen with *Ark Royal*, where she was expected to be she was not, and this time she was under repair. The convoy was dispersed. The *Empress* and *Strathaird* (the latter was in fact held up for about ten days for minor repairs) then proceeded unescorted because they were both capable of relatively high speeds. Nicholson remained on the *Empress* as a passenger, but still retained the appointment of Commodore.

He was leaving his cabin at the precise moment that Jope began dropping his bombs and machine-gunning the ship. It seemed to him that the closing of his cabin door, a bomb explosion, the air raid alarm and the machine and cannon fire all erupted at the same moment. From his cabin two decks below the navigation bridge he raced for the stairway by the officers' flat and up to the bridge where he first saw Mr Keay. He asked if the ship had been hit. Keay found time to grunt at the superfluous question.

'Look behind you, Commodore, Sir.'

The Captain was now back from the chartroom and Nicholson asked him if he should go down to the Wireless Room and instruct the operators to send out an alarm. Sapsworth did not answer. He was far too shocked by what had happened in those brief seconds, and most immediately he was concerned with the cannon shots which had ripped into his bridge and the inferno behind him where flame and smoke were towering up into the sky over his obliterated sports deck. The wireless operators knew what to do without being told.

But Nicholson did go down to the Wireless Room, and found an operator standing on the sports deck outside it trying to avoid the choking smoke. He explained that an SOS had been sent out in accordance with routine procedures, without awaiting orders. The nature of the attack, the time and the ship's position accompanied the call. An acknowledgement had been received within minutes and then, also as normal procedure, confirmation of the attack was made by radio telephone.

* * *

Mrs Rona Trotter was the wife of Captain Henry Trotter, an officer of the Sherwood Rangers (Notts Yeomanry), commanded by Lieutenant-Colonel Lord Yarborough in the Middle East. Reluctantly, like many others, Captain Trotter had seen his wife evacuated from Palestine when the Italians entered the war. She was sent to Port Suez to join a ship bound for South Africa or the United Kingdom; they were not sure which when they parted. Captain Trotter, who must have been an objective or perhaps just an apprehensive man, gave his wife £100 in cash, a flask of brandy and a loaded revolver, and with these assurances of economic, spiritual and bodily safety she had embarked on the *Empress* at Port Tewfik on 22 September 1940.

As it happened, her brother-in-law Major George Trotter of the Royal Scots Greys was on the same ship also going home after a three-year spell with the 7th Armoured Division of the British Army of the Nile. They had all expected an escort to nurse them to their destination, but at Cape Town their hopes were shattered. Nevertheless the voyage was a pleasant one with most of the luxuries and delights of a rambunctious and hilarious peacetime tour still available on a ship carrying only about one-third of its peacetime complement of passengers. The weather was beautiful, even as they approached the United Kingdom; the appointments and food were splendid, the service was bountiful and the company jolly. Everything, in fact, was lovely. Until 0920 on 26 October.

Mrs Trotter did not eat breakfast. This was a lifelong habit and during the voyage it had enabled her to enjoy a little more sleep and, as on this occasion, to get a few small jobs done which others had to do later or the night before. On this day at 0920 she was packing her luggage ready for disembarkation the next morning.

The shock of the bomb followed immediately by the rasp of the klaxons shook Mrs Trotter badly. She dashed from her cabin, half guessing what was happening but still hoping that it was not. In the alleyway she bumped into Colonel Stevenson of the Seaforth Highlanders who was bleeding from a face severely lacerated by flying splinters of shattered varnished panelling in his cabin.

'Christ!' he said, perhaps forgetting himself as he confronted the startled lady. 'That was a bloody bomb! It's an air raid!'

Mrs Trotter went back and grabbed her handbag complete

with its emergency kit of money, brandy and revolver. She wore a look of forthright determination. It was as though if she had come up against a brick wall she would have gone right through without noticing it. But immediately she found herself facing something more horrifying than a brick wall, for suddenly, cruelly, blankly, the lights went out. No flicker, no warning and she was surrounded by the proverbial Stygian gloom. But seconds later, such is the human body's capacity for dealing with most demands put upon it, she was able to discern the faintest of glimmers of light filtering through open cabin doors where, if the scuttles were not closed, enough light came through for her to pick out grey from black. Nevertheless her first impulse was to scream and panic—the popular expedient in such circumstances. Here she was, lost below decks, in the dark, in a ship which might be sinking.

But then came a hubbub of voices and a light. A group of stewards had come up from the dining rooms and were making their way to the boat deck. She attached herself to these men and remained with them almost until she eventually left the ship, a departure which would turn out to be a hazardous and adventurous one calling for a great deal of courage and endurance and which 45 years later she is inclined to depreciate.

* * *

Mrs Joan Stephenson (today Lady Stephenson of Hassop Green in Derbyshire), wife of Lieutenant-Colonel Stephenson of the Queen's Own Yorkshire Dragoons Yeomanry (not to be confused with the aforementioned Colonel Stevenson), had like Mrs Trotter been evacuated from the Middle East and was travelling unaccompanied on her way home. The regiments of both Colonel Stephenson and Captain Trotter belonged to the same brigade and the families knew one another. They came from adjacent parts of England and to this day those who survive are still friends, as are their progeny.

Lord Yarborough and Lady Nancye Yarborough were also passengers on the *Empress*, and they had promised Colonel Stephenson that they would look after his wife during the voyage in the same way that Major Trotter had promised to look after Mrs Rona Trotter, his sister-in-law.

Today, Lady Stephenson is a writer of charming, extremely

intelligent and informative letters. The present Lord Yarborough speaks of her in glowing terms. She was (in 1984) 83 years of age and the present Lady Yarborough's step-sister. She recalls that the then Lord and Lady Yarborough looked after her well and were in every way very kind. For example, at Cape Town, military Movement Control had arbitrarily transferred Mrs Stephenson to the *Franconia*, a ship which simply did not compare in any way, with the *Empress of Britain*, except that it floated. Indeed, as the author recalls, it was a ship which seemed always to have a list to starboard and when seen through the spray, mist, wind and grey water of a North Atlantic gale, looked positively dangerous. By the time the Earl heard the news, Mrs Stephenson's baggage had already been moved over and neither he nor his temporary ward liked the idea at all. The Earl did not mess about. He just went ashore, stamped all over Movement Control and within a couple of hours all was back as it should have been and the Earl, like the Duke of Wellington on the Eve of Waterloo as related by Stanley Holloway ('Sam! Sam! Pick oop thee moosket!') was muttering, 'Let voyage commence!'

On 25 October Joan Stephenson had forgotten to adjust her watch, so was late for breakfast the next morning. This was a meal she had shared during the voyage with a Mrs Wallace. After breakfast the two ladies would usually go to the sun deck and play tennis, but because Mrs Stephenson was late that particular morning Mrs Wallace went off on her own saying, 'I will wait for you on the sports deck'.

Some minutes later Oberleutnant Jope dropped his bombs, the sports deck had a large hole in it spewing forth smoke and flame, and Mrs Wallace was dead.

When the air raid alarm sounded, Mrs Stephenson left the table with a Mrs Morse, another lady whose husband served under Lord Yarborough. They mounted the stairs but soon found their way along a passage blocked by a watertight door which a steward had closed at the sounding of the alarm.

* * *

Mr William Stanley, Second Officer, was in his own cabin in the officers' quarters below the bridge. Like others he was not afterwards sure of the timing, but the way he remembered it was that the alarm went first and was followed immediately afterwards by the blast of a bomb. He scrambled into his uniform. In emergencies his duty was to proceed with dispatch to his air raid station on 'B' deck square, forward, the first class entrance. This was by the main stairway and opposite the bureau. He went by way of the Mall on the lounge deck where he met Mr Keay who, relieved on the bridge by Captain Sapsworth, was investigating damage, accompanied by the carpenter's mate. All three went out to the starboard side promenade intending to go to the Mayfair Lounge. However, both it and the adjacent ship's orderly room (the peacetime writing room) were blazing fiercely. They connected hoses from the fireboxes, ran them out and turned the valves. Only the barest trickle of water came through, a frightening forerunner to many similar experiences in all parts of the ship during that horrendous day.

Stanley's attempts to get back inside the ship by the revolving door between the Mayfair Lounge and the orderly room were frustrated by dust, smoke, flame and debris. Everything that could be wrong was wrong. He fought his way forward through the smoke along the promenade to the main stair entrance and again entered the Mall. Now he had to kick his way through debris to get to his station on 'B' deck square where his fire party should have assembled. He met some of his men halfway down the stair between 'A' and 'B' decks, and with them was the Sixth Officer, Mr Mansell. Stanley ordered them to assemble their gear and go to the promenade deck where the worst of the fires then appeared to be.

A number of servicemen were standing about on the promenade awaiting instructions, apparently unable to make their way to their boat stations. With them was a Chief Petty Officer bleeding badly from a wound in the head. Stanley ordered him down to the sick bay and the others to run hoses from 'A' deck up the stairway. Once again when the valve was turned the flow of water was negligible. They might as well have spat.

At this stage Mr Keay reappeared and he, as frustrated as Stanley, decided to climb back up to the bridge to explain to the Captain just how bad things were. Briefly, this was that the entire midships sections were hopelessly on fire, the Mayfair Lounge, the orderly room and the starboard side of the promenade were burning unchecked and uncheckable. There was virtually no water coming through from the mains and the entire area on and below deck was obscured by a choking pall of thick smoke. Many people had been injured and killed. Many lifeboats had been destroyed.

0935: 'Anyone know what's up?'

Seven decks below in the engine room Junior Second Engineer William Evans was engineer of the watch. He had begun his stint at 0800 and at that time all was well. Routinely, he sent his first and second assistants around the machinery spaces checking that everything was functioning correctly. He was prepared for an uneventful watch.

His first intimation that something was wrong came an hour later. This was an unusual and very heavy noise in the diesel room. It must have been the shock wave of Jope's first bomb exploding seven decks up in the Mayfair Lounge. But Evans did not know that.

He hurried into the diesel room, the compartment immediately forward of the foremost engine room on 'F' and 'G' decks. There was some airborne dust, fragments of asbestos and other material, but the diesels themselves were working normally with no evident damage. All Evans could think of was that something had gone wrong in the kitchens two decks up. Nevertheless he was worried.

Something was up. The times being what they were, his mind turned to thoughts of U-boats, torpedoes and mines, but there appeared to be nothing like that. He poked about for a few minutes and then returned to his station on 'F' deck, intending to call his Chief and contact the bridge. Back in the engine room his apprehension was given substance. There had been a request on the telegraph for full speed.

'Anyone know what's up?'

No one did. His assistants had opened up more nozzles.

As it turned out this request for more speed was the last order he was to receive on the telegraph, for very soon it was not working and there were loose wires hanging at the engine room end.

Evans was unable to raise his off-duty Chief on the telephone. He was more than worried now because to add to his troubles smoke was coming into the engine room and he did not know why. What did give him a clue was a telephone call from the kitchens asking for more pressure on the fire main. Briefly a song he had sung at school came to him: 'Fire in the galley, fire down below—let's get a bucket of water, boys, there's fire down below!'

Fire indeed! For by this time, 0940, there were fires not only in the kitchens but throughout the entire centre of the ship and what was needed above all else was water to put them out. But there was none—or at best, very little.

Evans could not understand what was wrong. As long as the generators were working there should have been adequate pressure. He had two sets of pumps, one for the sanitary system and the other for the fire services, and their combined capacity should have been a satisfactory 60 tons per hour. An extra pump had been put on as a precaution a few days ago when they entered the danger zone and the result was a pressure at the fire main of 60 lbs given at a height of 140 feet. All this when they had not needed it. And now when the pressure was on, so to speak, there was no pressure at all.

Further reports came through to clarify what was happening above. One said that there was water flooding the lower decks and this, coupled with the lack of pressure, sounded ominously to Evans like fractured mains. Irritably and with increasing edginess he watched as his men put on their gas-masks. Smoke was literally billowing through the engine room. Where was the Chief?

By 0945 they were in very bad trouble and still no one had really told Evans what was going on. Unable to contact the Chief Engineer he ordered an assistant to telephone the bridge explaining the appalling conditions in the engine room, and it was this call which apparently made Captain Sapsworth decide what to do.

* * *

On his way back from the Wireless Room, Commodore Nicholson heard more explosions and by the time he reached the bridge there was very little visible abaft of it. The whole ship from the bridge to the capstan deck was covered in smoke and flame. The explosions he heard are something of a mystery, for according to Oberleutnant Jope no strikes were made during his second attack and it must have been at the time of that attack that Nicholson returned to the bridge. Apparently the bomb, or bombs, dropped in that attack missed and went into the sea. Perhaps Nicholson mistook the firing of the 3-inch gun for bomb explosions, which seems remarkable. But in any case he was not the only one who heard unexplained explosions—or, let us say, unexplained at that time.

He reached the bridge between 0945 and 0950. Standing beside the bedevilled Captain, Nicholson saw the plane swing round from the perimeter of its circle and make once more for the ship.

'Looks as though he is going to have another go,' he said, and then the plane, coming in from ahead for the first time, opened up with its cannon, raking the forecastle, forewelldeck, the forward promenade and the bridge. Everyone ducked.

A split second later they heard the overpowering report of another massive explosion aft. Huge new volumes of smoke erupted. But it was the last of the attacks, for the German had dropped all his bombs. One of them hit the deck near the 6-inch gun, failed to explode and rolled off into the sea. Another of these 550-lb monstrosities hit the after promenade deck near the docking bridge, scoring a near direct hit on the 3-inch gun, scattering the gunners, ripping the docking bridge apart, smashing the nearby boom, and starting a fire on the after promenade. A lady was killed on the tennis court some hundred feet away, either by the bomb or by the cannon fire. Within minutes ammunition stored in the lockers on 'A' deck began to explode spontaneously.

By this time the Captain knew that his ship was burning virtually out of control. What else was there for him to do for the passengers' safety? Very little—except to tell them to get to their boats. Incredible though it seemed, after only half an hour of action it was now time to abandon. An hour ago it would have seemed beyond belief that this huge ship could be so quickly destroyed. The truth now facing Captain Sapsworth must have seemed as unbelievable as that confronting the Captain of the unsinkable *Titanic* 28 years before.

Having made the decision, he was confronted with what might be called ancillary hazards. Apart from his siren he had no means of communicating with other parts of the ship except the engine room, and then only by telephone. How was he to instruct the boat crews that their boats could not stop at the embarkation deck because it was burning? Not only would passengers be unable to reach the boats on that deck, but the boats themselves would be burned if they stopped there. And if the boats were lowered directly to the water while the ship was still under way they would simply drift astern before passengers could embark. He might put the engines in reverse to slow the ship, but that would mean keeping the engineers down in the engine room. And the engine room was already untenable.

'Oh, my God . . .!'

He made his decisions because he had to.

*   *   *

When the Captain came through to the navigating bridge to assume command, Howell picked up a portable telephone and went down the stairway to the officers' quarters and along the passage in an attempt to get to the promenade deck and the areas of the fires to see exactly what was going on.

The stair from the officers' flat was damaged, obstructed by debris and overladen with smoke. Nevertheless, he eventually reached the doorway to the first class entrance. Here he found several injured people, among them a soldier with a broken leg. Howell put his telephone down, grasped the soldier under the armpits and dragged him into the Mall to get him away from the smoke.

There was a great deal of screaming and shouting going on. To overcome the smoke problem he pulled on his gas-mask and plunged along the promenade towards the fires. The orderly room was already an inferno. Beyond he entered the midships first class entrance through the revolving doors to the lobby outside the Mayfair Lounge. Inside the raw flames dominated—high, fierce and seemingly with a gloating, triumphant euphoria like a genie bottled up for a thousand years suddenly released to wreak vengeance upon everything. The smoke reeked sickeningly of burning varnish. An injured woman lay screwed up in a corner. She was bloody, her clothes had been partially ripped off by the bomb blast and she was screaming for help. By her side lay a soldier, his body grotesquely twisted, either unconscious or dead.

Howell picked the woman up and half carried, half led her out through the double door, told her to cover her face and then rushed her screaming through the lobby. The lights had gone out and the place was thick with smoke, black as a claustrophobic nightmare. He stumbled over bodies and debris towards the daylight coming through the revolving doors.

Outside he took her forward through the smoke, dodging the licking flames from the orderly room and sat her down near a stairway outside the Mall. She was crying for her husband.

'He's *there—there* . . . don't you understand? He'll die . . . Go and help him . . .'

It was the blind unreasoning command of a woman distraught. And Howell reminded himself that he had only just got *her* out by the skin of his teeth. There was little more he could do, but he had to try.

Back at the entrance door outside the Mayfair Lounge lobby he found it impossible to enter. It was belching out harsh, sooty smoke which burned his face even through the gas-mask. Moreover, the rubber itself was a hazard, so he wrenched it off.

A fire-fighting party had rigged up a hose and he went to help them, taking a fire-extinguisher from a box. His extinguisher petered out within seconds and when the fire party opened the valve of the hose only a trickle of water came out. Howell saw all this as a portent of doom, for he knew then that there was no way out for the *Empress*. He could only guess at the complacency of those responsible for the failures, knowing that somewhere there must have been culpabilities. But at that time he did not know that the first bomb had fractured the fire fighting water mains.

Now he made his way back to where he had left the woman on the promenade deck, intending to offer some hopeless hope for her husband. He could neither see her nor approach the spot where he had left her and his face whitened as he remembered his responsibility.

* * *

Only a matter of 30 minutes earlier, and like a million sea travellers before him, Chief Petty Officer Herbert Burley RN had been staring fascinated at the tons of water being thrown back by the cleaving bows. He was leaning on the rail smoking a cigarette, on the starboard side of the forward promenade. Well aware of the dangers in those waters, he wore his lifejacket at all times, in his case the blue inflatable type, RN issue. He stared relaxedly into the heaving waters unaware that the enemy was above him and only seconds away.

Out of the blue came the rattle of machine-gun fire. He noted the reflected flash of the 3-inch gun on the water and just for one brief moment thought no more of it than that the after gunners were practicing. Then the gunners above him opened up with their Lewis guns and the overpowering roar of a four-engined bomber pulsed deafeningly overhead. Then he was running and shouting, 'Take cover! It's an air raid!'

He did not remember much of that run along the deck but suddenly he was at the forward first class entrance. A bomb exploded some 40 yards aft and the blast crashed the door back into his face, stunning him, and he stumbled to his knees.

The plane passed. The guns were still firing and he heard the crackling of the klaxons. Shortly, he arose and entered the foyer. The lights were out and the only illumination came from the doorways on either side. The air, heavy with smoke, reeked of explosive. Women and children were screaming and the groans of the injured came to him as though from a deep black well. Someone called, 'Oh, my head . . .'

Burley groped towards the voice and struck a match. Halfway down the stairs the Officer Commanding Troops, Lieutenant-Colonel Jackson, lay badly wounded. Burley called for help and a petty officer named Farmer joined him. The CPO sent him away to find a stretcher but it was very dark and Farmer decided to go below to his cabin for a torch. Later he and Burley found a broken door. They placed Colonel Jackson on it and took him to the sick bay on 'C' deck.

Burley left Farmer to handle the admission and went forward through the gloom. The sound of the klaxons came faintly over the speakers and he thought that unless a man were near a speaker, he would not hear. It all seemed a bit pathetic and he, like others, gave thought to what seemed the state of unreadiness for real emergency in which the ship was maintained. But like others he did not know the full story, part of which was that the communications system had been badly damaged and that in some parts of the ship it no longer existed at all.

At the well over the *Jacques Cartier* he looked down about 30 feet wondering if anyone were still down there, hurt but hidden by the smoke.

* * *

The Purser, Mr Pearch, was enjoying himself on the sports deck sucking in the sparkling air, so exhilarating that he felt he could almost bite on it. On the other hand, he was wishfully thinking of the opulent, piping days of peace, for truthfully he did not really like travelling on a half empty ship—it was altogether too easy and certainly not purposeful enough for this energetic gentleman. The other thing he did not like was the nagging uncertainty of travel through these highly danger-ous waters where at any moment he and his ship could be blown sky high.

But there were only a few more hours at sea, and then some days ashore and at home, although he had no doubt he would have to spend most of the time mending blackout screens, gardening and sleeping at night under the dining room table or, even worse, in that abominable, damp and earthy Anderson shelter at the bottom of the garden where the bird bath used to be. He grimaced, thinking of the rather splendid bed in his cabin. The Company did him well, no doubt about that. But there it was. He would be on leave and mostly with his family, although there would also be the chore of preparing for the next trip. He did not like thinking about 'next trips' under these wartime conditions, and thoughts of another grim, grey departure into hazardous winter seas from Seaforth docks or the Clyde were to be put aside.

Here, high up above the overhanging promenade deck he stared out at the grey October sea. He was alert and, like everyone else on board, occupied his time at the rail keeping an eye open for a periscope. His lifejacket was tied around him and his shoes were unlaced. But despite all this, when he heard the machine-gun fire he dismissed it abstractedly as practice. He had heard it often before. Extraordinarily, although he was surprised, even the deafening roar of a huge low-flying plane did not immediately bring home the truth to him. What did was the concussion of the huge bomb striking the deck somewhere towards the stern.

He was 250 feet forward of the explosion which followed in the Mayfair Lounge, but still he was knocked off his feet. He crouched there getting used to the ugly truth. From somewhere forward he faintly heard the klaxons. He stood up. There were things he had to do. He was dizzy as he staggered along the short length of deck to the stairway by the children's playground.

Immediately he had to get to the bureau in the first class entrance of 'B' deck square. In an emergency it was his responsibility to collect all papers, cash and valuables in the ship's care, put them in canvas bags and take them wherever he went. When that was done he was supposed to help passengers, directing them to their boat stations if 'Abandon Ship Stations' was sounded or, as in this case, persuade them that the best thing they could do until otherwise instructed was to lie down flat on the deck under cover.

Mr Pearch's office was some distance down. He had to get to the Mall, along to the main staircase and then down two decks. The head of the stairs on the promenade deck was thick with scattered debris. There was no light except that coming through the prom deck windows. He stumbled over the blackened and apparently lifeless body of a soldier. Nearby a sergeant-major lay with injured legs but still conscious and able to ask for help. Pearch called two soldiers and together they carried the man to the lift near the revolving door. Here they lay him down and went to find a stretcher. In the end they had to hoist him on to their shoulders, and thus they carried him to the sick bay.

The stairs here in the Mall were a mess. The only light came through the doors and someone came groping towards Pearch with a torch. People were shouting for stretchers. Everyone was coughing, from the smoke. He wondered why there were no fire parties on hand.

On 'B' deck he went into his personal office and, perhaps from some trained-in instinct to look his best even under the worst circumstances, he tied his shoe-laces and put on his coat and cap. Then his regained *savoir-faire* was shattered by another massive explosion seemingly just over his head. He ducked and looked at the ceiling apprehensively. It was another bomb attack. He wondered how many more there would be.

One of the surprising things is that between the first blast which had knocked Pearch to his knees and this latter explosion, half an hour had passed yet to him it seemed no time at all. His journey from the sports deck to the bureau and the episode with the wounded serjeant-major had passed like a flash.

* * *

The Chief Steward's cabin, or rather his suite, was on the starboard side of 'D' deck, a little forward of midships. It was probably one of the most comfortable situations on the ship, being in the area of least movement. Which, of course, was why the first class dining rooms, one of his major concerns, were also in this area, being places where passengers would be least threatened by seasickness.

Just before 0920 the Chief Steward, Mr Lawrence Moss, had been leaving his suite. Like others below he did not hear the air raid alarm. Or perhaps what really happened was that being pre-occupied with the duties of this trip, he heard but did not identify the signal. Later he said he had heard some whistling noises on the intercom, but he paid no attention to them. Not, that is, until a few moments later, when there was a resounding thump above his head. He ducked and screwed his eyes up. Then he heard a second thump and a horrifying concussion as the ship shuddered, heeling over sharply as it turned at dramatic speed.

'My God,' he thought, 'we've been torpedoed.'

Briefly his head span as he tried to assemble in his mind all the things he had to do, and not only the things *he* had to do but those he had to make sure others under his authority did. One of these was to ensure that his stewards closed all the fireproof and watertight doors and scuttles. Fortunately watertight doors had officially been closed ever since they entered the danger area at 10° north of the Equator, and so had the scuttles on the lower decks. But still, crewmen were wont to open them in the course of their cabin and alleyway duties and sometimes they forgot to close them again.

But the firedoors were different, and if things were going according to routine his stewards would already be setting about the job of closing them, evacuating passengers to the lounge deck and making sure none were left below. Then they should report to him in the foyer before the main stair on this deck. It was his job to report to the Captain by telephone when he was confident that all had been done that should have been done. He awaited the routine reports anxiously. Smoke was creeping down the stairway and the smell of burning wood and varnish disturbed him. He could only guess what had happened.

The next 15 minutes were confusing. Of the stewards who were to report to him only four did so, so he could not be sure

45

that everything which should have been done had been done. For all he knew there might still be passengers and stewards trapped below decks and nothing he could do about it. He let his report to the Captain hang over. It was no use reporting that he had nothing to report. In any case he would not have been able to contact the Captain.

In the kitchens the staff were behaving admirably, and had already run out hoses between the first class and tourist dining rooms wherein the smoke was increasing rapidly—as though its source were being fuelled. The fire smell was strong, the screaming from the main stairway frightening.

Moss helped the men with the hoses, straightening them out and stretching them towards hydrants. But when the hydrants were opened, after the first gush of water, the flow died away to a trickle. He guessed what had happened to the mains. His telephone call to the engine room produced only a mumbled reply which he did not understand. He did not know that whoever it was speaking was doing so through a gas-mask.

He mustered the gathering passengers into some sort of order, trying to reassure them. What he really wanted was for someone to reassure *him*. These people were bewildered, some of them querulous and demanding, all of them fearful. He tried to speak normally, pretending that there was little urgency, but the smoke and the shouting from the stairway belied his efforts. No one wanted to listen to him being calm.

On 'D' deck square he hoped an up-draught at the stairwell would help clear the air, but he had forgotten that one of the physical properties of smoke is that mostly it is heavier than air and a lot of it goes *down*. He wondered if he should take his passengers to the upper outer decks so that they could breath more easily.

* * *

Major George Trotter, who, it will be remembered, was brother-in-law to Mrs Rona Trotter, had been striding in a most masculine manner up and down the sun deck with Lieutenant-Colonel Lord Yarborough. Colonel Yarborough and his wife Lady Nancye had been feeling splendid, vigorous and bristling with ozone-induced good health and looking forward to a stay, no matter how short, amidst the comfortable grandeur and rusticity of the Yarborough family seat at Brocklesbury Park in Lincolnshire.

Then the crack of bullets ripping up the deck and the rattle of light machine-gun fire had stopped them in their tracks. There was a thunderous roar as a huge four-engined aircraft swept over them. They flung themselves to the deck in the approved manner and Trotter had just the flicker of a sight of a massive bomb flying over the tennis court. The following blast and eruption of smoke lifted up the deck as though it were made of stretched rubber. Then the plane had gone, machine-gunning the bridge as it passed and veering towards the starboard side.

They had heard no alarm.

Standing up to lean over the rail, they watched the plane circle away to starboard a mile or so ahead. The ship was swinging dramatically to port, thrashing her stern through the water. The plane crossed her bows well ahead and returned along the port side, machine-gunning as it came until it was once more astern.

In those moments Yarborough and Trotter made for the shelter of the 'special' sun deck cabins abreast of the after funnel. The entrance was through a café and this had been damaged making Trotter suppose, as did many others, that at least two bombs had fallen—the one which went through the deck amidships and the other near the café.

Inside the alleyway all was dark. They returned the way they had come and made for the port side companion, trying to get down to the open promenade deck. There was a great deal of burning debris.

At this stage the plane had come in for its second attack. They flung themselves to the deck once more, opened their mouths wide and squeezed their eyes shut in the approved manner for this sort of thing. The bomb did not arrive. It missed the ship altogether, exploding harmlessly in the sea.

The smoke emerging from the entrance to the 'special' cabins in dirty brown gusts sped them on their way downwards. On the promenade they entered the ante-room of the Cathay Lounge and so to the after stairway.

Down on 'A' deck square they decided to make their way forward and *en route* along the alleyway Lord Yarborough somehow disappeared and Trotter saw no more of him on the *Empress of Britain*. Lady Nancye also seemed to have departed, no one knew where. In any event, Trotter had quite enough to do to look after himself in the blinding smoke and darkness, for now the lights along the 'A' deck alleyway had gone out. But he continued to grope forward, at last reaching the main stairs.

On the stairs he bumped into a Lieutenant-Commander Garrett. Garrett was assisting a badly wounded man and he asked Trotter to take over and get this man to the sick bay on 'C' deck. Two men standing by found a board and using this as a stretcher they struggled down the stairs and eventually got the man to the hospital, which was busy and working with difficulty under emergency lighting. There were many wounded and many shocked.

After delivering his man, Trotter made his way aft, sensing that he would be in the way hanging about the sick bay. At the after stairway he rested against the bulkhead of the operating theatre, and stayed here until another bomb fell at about 0950.

The terrifying thump came out of the semi-darkness and was followed by the explosion overhead. It seemed that its centre was a little abaft his position. It must have been very close because the concussion stunned him. By the time he had recovered his wits, a crowd of frightened people had come up from 'D' deck. They said the lower decks were flooding and Trotter supposed that the ship had been holed. He smothered his own panic, trying to calm them down more by example than by anything credibly reassuring he could say such as, for example, that 'it would be alright, the crew knew what they were doing'. He settled himself nervously on the stairs, apprehensive and with a claustrophobic urge to get to the open decks above.

When the thick, brown and yellow smoke surged downwards, reeking with the nauseating stench of burning varnish, he gave up and headed the party through it up the stairs. Abaft the tourist stairs on 'A' deck he now heard repeated explosions and at first supposed that the plane was still attacking. Later he discovered that these were spontaneous explosions of the 6-inch ammunition in the magazine. Then, for some unexplained reason, it appears that he decided to go one level down again to 'B' deck. Maybe he supposed that if the 'A' deck magazine went up, the explosion would be upwards! Safer to be below.

* * *

There was something special about Lieutenant-Commander Charles Garrett, of the Royal Navy, as we shall see. He was in charge of a naval draft which had embarked at Suez. The draft had then consisted of 267 men, but it had been split up at Durban and Cape Town and dispersed throughout several ships, leaving Garrett with only 78 officers and men.

For some reason which is not clear, Garrett had assumed or been appointed to many tasks during the voyage and he seems to have had responsibility for more things than anyone else. Whether he had picked up these special responsibilities by force of character as they arose, or had been appointed to them either by the Captain or the OC Troops, it is impossible now to say. Certainly, by the nature of the questions put to him at the Board of Enquiry which was to come, the special report he put in after the action and the things he did after landing survivors at Gourock, it did appear either that he had a tremendous sense of personal responsibility and a governing need to get things done right, or else he had these things thrust upon him.

For example, although he was to all intents and purposes just in transit and incidentally in charge of a small group of men also in transit, the question put to him by the Board, 'What means did you use of fighting the fire in the first instance?', seems to imply that he had responsibility for fire-fighting, although such responsibility is certainly not a draft commander's—unless especially detailed—but that of the ship's Chief Officer and his subordinates.

In any event, according to his report and the evidence he gave verbally, he took a very active part in what went on as regards not only fire-fighting but also the mustering of passengers, getting wounded people to the sick bay, the construction of rafts, being in charge of the guns, getting passengers to obey orders, loading them into lifeboats, giving orders to those already in charge of lifeboats, the arrangements for air raid precautions and for dealing with any planes which might attack the ship, and generally giving a great many orders to a great many people. All of which was fair enough if there was a deficiency in leadership. Someone had to fill the gap if that were so—someone who *could* lead and who knew what he was doing.

But what is surprising is that whilst several of the crew and others received 'Mentions' or other awards as a result of this action, Lieutenant-Commander Garrett got nothing in the Board findings but an agreement with his recommendations (about which they found nothing exceptional or new) and an acknowledgement that there was nothing wrong with the way he and his men did their job.

One gets the feeling that Garrett might have been a bit pushy, critical of his superior officers, and perhaps even looking for a decoration and thereby, as sometimes may happen, negating any chance he had of getting one. The fact is that there is an element of criticism of the ship's officers' and crew's behaviour in Garrett's evidence and report, and this would not have endeared him to the senior officers who comprised the Board.

Before that fatal day, Garrett had looked after his men well, ensuring that they received their pay and tobacco issues when the draft was split up. As regards the security of the ship, in the event of enemy action he had conferred with the Captain upon action necessary should there be an air raid. But why Garrett? There is no record of his being asked for his opinion or, except perhaps as the result of his own initiative, being appointed to a position where his opinion would have been sought.

In his personal report he says: 'Sea Transport Officer, Suez, requested *me* to embark 1,000 women and children on the morning of the 23rd. These were army families bound for South Africa or the United Kingdom. *I* embarked these with Naval draft at Port Tewfik (Port Suez) on the 22nd.'

In other words, *he*, simply a naval draft commander, embarked these passengers a day before he says the STO asked him to. It is very odd indeed. Quite apart from the time anomaly, why would the STO have consulted with *him* about army families when there was an army Officer Commanding Troops on board, fully equipped with an Adjutant and a permanent ship's staff. It would have been extraordinary.

Then, on 23 September on leaving Port Suez, he says, '*I* manned the AA gun' (presumably the 3-inch high-angle gun) 'and the 6-inch gun belonging to the ship'. But the gunners themselves were to say that they had no knowledge of any officer being in charge of them, and they did not see any officer present at their practice shoots. Furthermore, there was a CPO, Royal Navy, in charge of the DEMS permanent ship's gunners who had been in charge of the guns and the crews for several months. There is no suggestion as far as is known, and neither is it probable, that this Chief Petty Officer (Jevans) suddenly found himself to be working under orders from Commander Garrett, an officer in transit. Some naval ratings belonging to Garrett's draft did, in fact supplement the DEMS permanent gun crews under command of CPO Jevans.

But on 24 September, Garrett—he says—had requested the Master and the Commodore (who was then still an active participant in the conduct of the convoy) to carry out air raid drill. Note that he was not ordered to do this and neither, apparently, was he approached on the matter. *Garrett* simply requested the Master and the Commodore, and they had simply complied. Again, it is very odd.

Then, apparently feeling that discipline and organization were not as tight as they should have been, he, off his own bat, made out what he called an 'organization' and orders for the drill and air raid precautions. When, he says, he presented these to the Captain they were adopted and he was allowed to put his 'organization' into practice. One wonders what the Officer Commanding Troops and his staff must have thought about all this.

Garrett was conscious that Italy was now in the war. One gets the feeling that he supposed no one else knew this. *He* therefore expected on the passage through the Red Sea, an air attack from Massawa, the port for what was then Italian Eritrea. But nothing happened and the convoy reached Durban without incident.

During the voyage normal boat drills were carried out. This was routine stuff which whilst complying with Board of Trade requirements (by then 'Sea Transport') and giving the troops and other passengers something to do, also kept them alive to unpleasant possibilities and ensured that they might know what to do should there be an emergency.

One of the extraordinary things about the action was that there was apparently no one, army, navy, air force or merchant marine, on board the ship who could recognize a Focke-Wulf Condor sideways on as an enemy plane, even at middle distance. But despite this extraordinary deficiency there were still certain things to guide their actions should a plane approach, and these things should have been a safeguard.

Garrett says that he told the Captain as follows (and the words are Garrett's own): 'If any aircraft approached without identification, or under 1,000 feet with its wheels down, or if they were in formation, they should be stepped down, then he was entitled to regard such aircraft as enemy and open fire.'

Of this instruction *in toto* surely one is entitled to ask 'What on earth does that mean?' Certainly, breaking it up a bit, 'If any aircraft approached without identification or under 1,000 feet . . . then he was entitled to regard it as enemy and open fire' makes sense. But what is all this about 'with its wheels down, or if they were in formation, they should be stepped down'? It might be that friendly planes were instructed to lower their wheels to show they were friendly, but it would be most remarkable if an enemy plane would be flying about with its wheels down just to show that it *was* an enemy. The business about 'or if they were in formation, they should be stepped down' in the context is equally confusing. One suspects that Garrett might have been trying to roll off his tongue an instruction he had learned by rote too quickly and got that member twisted.

In any event, the Board of Enquiry accepted the repetition of what Garrett had said that he had told the Captain without question. One is entitled to wonder if they were really listening or perhaps if they were just tolerating him. But apparently at the outset of the voyage when Garrett *had* approached the Captain, Sapsworth had listened to what he had to say and *had* to some extent demurred. Garrett says that the Captain's words were: '. . . on previous voyages, aircraft had approached and not identified itself.' Hardly good grammar perhaps, but the meaning is quite clear.

Garrett had apparently then asked Captain Sapsworth how long ago that had been, and was told that it was during the outward voyage. This would have been within the previous three months. Garrett must then have grunted a bit for he says he told Captain Sapsworth that he thought things had changed at home by that time, 'as he had had a lot to do with anti-aircraft in his last ship' and he knew the instructions he had given were very recent. He then got the Captain to pin his instructions up on the chartroom wall. All of which seems to suggest that, in spite of faulty articulation, Commander Garrett saw himself as, or was seen to be, rather more than just a draft commander.

At about 0920 Garrett had heard the air raid alarm almost simultaneously with the concussion of a bomb explosion. He was down on 'D' deck at the time and did not at first realize what had happened and, whilst believing that there had been an attack on the ship, he supposed it to have been by torpedo.

One would suppose that if he had really believed himself to be in charge of the guns aft he would have found his way in that direction immediately. But he didn't. A few minutes later he was mounting the main stairs. Here he found heavy smoke already choking the promenade vestibule and a great deal of panic. From what he was then told he realized that the attack had come from the air and that 40 yards abaft of him a fierce fire was blazing in the Mayfair Lounge. His thought then was to go aft to the fire and help where he could, but lights were out in the vestibule and through the gloom he saw several wounded lying on the deck. He picked one of these men up and began helping him towards the stairs where he intended to take him down to the sick bay on 'C' deck. As we have seen, he met Major Trotter on the stairs and handed the injured man over to him.

On 'B' deck square he found a group of very worried people who wanted to know what was going on. Among them was a Captain Black of the Argyll and Sutherland Highlanders. Garrett instructed Black (one notes how he appears to take charge in every situation) to muster these people where they were, keep them lying on the deck and await further instructions.

There was no fire on 'B' deck at that time but there was a lot of smoke spreading downwards from the stairwell. Nevertheless it is remarkable how quickly the fire did spread, and the interior of the upper midships section had become an inferno within minutes.

Somehow, at about 0935, Garrett emerged at the promenade entrance outside the Mayfair Lounge and was calling for volunteers among the naval personnel to fight the fires. Men from all services came forward to run hoses out and do what they could with a shortage of water. At least for the next 35 minutes, with short breaks, Garrett was with these parties. During that time he saw no sign of the ship's officers or members of the crew in fire-fighting parties. At some time during this period Garrett tried to get to the guns but because of the fires on the promenade deck he was unable to do this.

The guns began firing again just before 0950. By that time Garrett had left the fire-fighting parties to try to get below to find out what had happened to the pumps. On 'C' deck, outside the sick bay, he met CPO Ransome who had been slightly wounded. It was whilst Garrett was with Ransome that the bomb which destroyed the 3-inch gun fell and shattered the tennis court and docking bridge above them. What remained of the lighting on 'C' deck went out and Garrett, sensing a rising panic about him, told the assembled passengers in the alleyway to hold hands and move forward. They did this and Ransome went with them.

* * *

Chief Petty Officer Frederick Ransome was the Chief in general charge of the naval draft assisting Lieutenant-Commander Garrett. When the attack came he had been standing by in the orderly room. Like others his first thought on hearing the gunfire was that the gunners were practicing. The explosion in the Mayfair Lounge, virtually only a few yards away, knocked him to the deck. Back on his feet he found that there was a severe cut on his forehead. He did not know if it was caused by the blast or from banging his head on the deck.

Already the orderly room was choking with explosion fumes, and smoke was rolling through the after doorway. Outside in the entrance hall a mass of debris was overhung by smoke and dust and the flicker of fire. Passengers picking themselves up were bewildered by the suddenness of it. There was some hysteria and screaming. Fires in the lounge quickly blazed upwards and out into the entrance lobby as the draught sucked the flames through. It was just a hint of what was to come.

Ransome left the orderly room and crossed to the stairs, making for the sick bay. On his way he stumbled over a woman's body. She was not badly hurt but very frightened and incapable of helping herself. Ransome picked her up and took her down with him to the sick bay.

On 'C' deck square he passed a mixed crowd of military, naval and civilian passengers all awaiting some instruction as to what to do next. At the sick bay a nurse took his charge away, then shortly afterwards came back to help him, bandaging his head. This must have been one of the Queen Alexandra's Imperial Military Nursing Service sisters who were travelling as passengers.

At this stage Garrett arrived and seeing the bandage asked

him if he was all right. One can imagine the conversation which may have ensued.

'I'm okay. Bit shaken. What's going on, sir?'

'I don't know. Looks like a right cock-up to me. There's a big fire up topside and no water. I'm trying to find out what happened to the pumps. Have you seen any of the ship's fire parties?'

But Ransome had not. The time must have been about 0950 because it was at this stage that the bomber struck again.

Such lights as there were along 'C' deck passage went out, panic was in the air and might easily have prevailed. Women were whimpering and clutching crying children. From the sick bay, where emergency lighting cast some light on the gloom, someone shouted, 'Keep calm!' It was probably Garrett who saved the day when he gave the order for all who could to move forward in the dark, holding one another's hands.

It took them some time to organize themselves and then they began worming their way through barely seen doorways, stairs and alleyways, most of them hitherto unknown and unexplored, but at last they arrived at the main stairs. Here clouds of smoke threatened them and again panic might easily have taken over. It was fortunate that Mr Metcalfe, the third class head steward, arrived. He had a torch and he took charge, leading the crocodile along the port side alleyway. Few of them had much idea where they were going, but they recognized competence and authority in Metcalfe and did as he told them.

Metcalfe led them through the crew's quarters and at last to the bottom of flights of stairs which took them up several decks to 'A' deck just forward of No 1 hatch on the forewelldeck.

Behind them they now saw the stark horror of the blazing bridge. A blinding, bubbling column of riotous smoke over-hung the ship and the sea like an immense, rolling fog. Ransome was still with them and was struggling to keep in check an almost overwhelming urge to run—to go *anywhere*, anywhere at all to get away from the ship and the flames which were smothering her. But, of course, there was nowhere to go.

* * *

Dr Edmund Delorme was a Canadian from Hamilton, Ontario. In November 1939, he had been trying to get to the United Kingdom to take his fellowship in surgery at Edinburgh, in spite of the war, but there were difficulties. The only way he could get a passage was to sign on as a ship's surgeon. He was appointed to the *Empress of Britain*. Here he found that he, practically alone, had replaced the entire medical staff of two doctors, one dentist and half a dozen nurses and orderlies, the permanent ones having all resigned at the outbreak of war.

In the United Kingdom, unable to relinquish his appointment, he had had perforce to stay with the *Empress*, had gone to New Zealand via the Middle East and back via the Cape; then again to Suez and once more back via the Cape. By this time he had vague ideas of unloading the appointment by signing on in the Royal Navy.

On this last voyage from Suez there were three other doctors on board as passengers—Major W. L. Greig, Royal Army Medical Corps, Colonel H. S. Peake, also RAMC, and one other, name unknown and probably a naval officer; there were also three sisters of the Queen Alexandra's Imperial Military Nursing Service, Sisters Horrocks, Dobson and Smith, and other ranks from the RAMC, Staff Serjeant Creed, Corporal Anthony and Corporal Marlow. Also there were the civilian dispenser, Mr Prout, and the sick bay attendant, Mr Newberry. So, all in all, for a complement of about 650 persons, Dr Delorme was not too badly off for medical staff should an emergency arise.

At about 0915 he had already been up for an hour or so, had exercised up on the sports deck, showered, dressed and eaten his breakfast. He had then stopped momentarily at his suite on the way to the sick bay which was one deck down on 'C' deck, on the port side. This was the only casualty station on the ship which, in view of its size, was perhaps strange. But then perhaps no one had yet had the action-incentive to get around to thinking such things out—hardly an excuse!—and organizing properly for an emergency. It was still early on in the war (after more than a year?) and Dr Delorme was not yet experienced in medicine at sea during an action. Later on, in the sphere of submarine warfare, he was to have a surfeit of it! The fact was that he did a remarkable job when required and in the event those who died would hardly have been saved by any number of casualty stations. The question still arises, however—what would have happened had there been 4,000 troops and families on board (as there could easily have been) instead of about 650? But the question is academic because no doubt had there been 4,000 the medical facilities would have been greatly increased before embarkation.

As Dr Delorme remembers events, at 0920 the klaxons had sounded. These were followed almost instantaneously by the crash and concussion of at least one bomb. The noise stunned him, thundering through the ship from somewhere forward. He knew perfectly well what had happened and he knew where he should be. He reached the sick bay within minutes and found Prout and Newberry already there setting up the theatre to receive casualties. They were cool and efficient. The wounded soon began to arrive. One of them, a steward, had suffered a compound fracture of the left thigh. Delorme immobilized the limb in a Thomas extension splint and the man was taken up to the boat deck ready to be put into a lifeboat should the situation develop. The next few hours were busy ones for Dr Delorme and his staff.

* * *

One member of the naval draft was a Lieutenant-Commander Harry Baker. He had been allotted no special duties except that at muster stations drill he was to be in charge of the passengers on the port side of the boat deck, assisting the inexperienced with their lifejackets and keeping them in order. Since boat stations had only taken place twice since leaving Durban, he had not had a lot to do.

At 0920 Baker had just finished his breakfast in the *Salle Montcalm*, a small dining room on the port side of the main *Salle Jacques Cartier*. Like most passengers below, he did not hear the alarm or, perhaps to clarify that, whilst he did hear something on the intercom, like the Chief Steward he did not interpret it as an air raid alert. But the blast of the bomb was, so to speak, self-definitive.

Baker left the *Montcalm* in a hurry and a little at a loss as to know what to do until instructed. He followed standing orders, however, and lay down on the floor waiting, as it were, for the next lot. Nothing happened immediately. He stood up and

made for the screaming and shouting coming from the stairway. Near the stairs he met a steward who was stumbling
along heroically supporting a comrade whose legs had been
badly hurt and who could not walk, probably the man with the
fractured thigh. Baker took one of his arms and placed it
around his neck.

'What's going on?'

'God only knows, sir. It's an air raid, that's all I know. Bomb
right down the funnel. Blown everything sky high. Incendiary.
It's all alight up there.' He jerked his head backwards.

Stories of bombs going down funnels are popular amongst
survivors of air attack at sea. Often it is not true, but does
seem to fit when a heavy bomb fails to explode on impact and
goes through several decks before doing so. It was not correct
in this case for Major Trotter, amongst others, had seen one
bomb strike the sun deck and go through and another near the
sun deck cabins, but none down the funnel. However, the idea
was an intriguing one which added unnecessary drama to what
was already a surfeit.

They climbed up to 'C' deck and to the sick bay. The lights
flickered repeatedly during their journey. Now they went out
for good. By contrast, the emergency lighting in the sick bay
showed them just how difficult things had become. Smoke
filled the air and everyone was coughing. There seemed to be
no escape.

After seeing the steward and his mate to the sick bay, Baker
went aft and climbed the tourist stairway to 'B' deck where he
knew the shelter deck abaft the after lounge would give him
air and a chance to see what was going on. He was scarcely at
the 'B' deck level when someone shouted that the bomber was
coming back. He fell to the deck, hunching his shoulders and
squeezing his eyes tight shut.

The explosion was devastating. He did not know where but
the bomb must have hit very near him. There were no lights
and when he had quieted his churning stomach nerves he arose
and groped through the after lounge towards the capstan deck.
Some stewards went with him.

★ ★ ★

Mr Alan Morison was Third Officer. He had been sharing the
forenoon watch with the Sixth Officer, Mr George Mansell,

but at breakfast time they had been relieved by the First Officer and the Fourth. This was routine.

They were seated together in the *Salle Wolfe* on the starboard side of 'D' deck, when the first bomb seemed to explode directly over their heads. Mansell thought it was like being hit with a muffled sledge hammer. Debris fell about them, speckling their heads and shoulders with white dust. Their first thoughts were of torpedoes and U-boats.

The klaxons rasped faintly through the intercom. Morison said, 'That means us!', and they headed forward towards the main stair. They scarcely gave a glance at an injured man lying on the stair for it was already obvious that the ship was in trouble with heavy smoke coming down the stairwell and there were things they had to do. They heard the ship's light machine-guns blazing away like kettle drums five decks up as they climbed towards them.

On the bridge they joined Captain Sapsworth and the Chief Officer who had also just arrived. The relieving officers of the watch, Keay and Howell, were recovering from the initial cannon attack, and from the chartroom they could see the thick pall of black smoke rolling over the decks, obscuring everything abaft the centre funnel.

The Captain, as we have seen, had relieved Mr Keay who, with his junior, Mr Howell, shortly afterwards disappeared down the stairs abaft the officers' flat. Morison was brushed aside and told to standby. He went into the wheelhouse and took up a position beside a quartermaster.

The Chief Officer, Mr Davies, snapped at Mansell, wanting to know what the hell he was doing on the bridge.

'It's my watch, Sir.'

'You're relieved. Get to your fire station.'

'Sir!'

He proceeded smartly to his station on 'B' deck square near the bureau and found some of his men there. There was no flame on 'B' deck at that time but the smoke was rolling in billows along the alleyway. In the absence of further instructions his party prepared its hoses, laying them out flat about the deck. There were further explosions, one of them a very heavy one, and it was shortly afterwards that they faintly heard the whistle booming continuously, telling them that the ship was being abandoned.

Mansell dismissed the fire party and ordered them to their

boat stations. He did not know if they got there, at any rate
not for some days. At least one of them was drowned and his
body found floating some hours afterwards about a mile away
from the ship. Today, Mansell says, 'To this day I do not
remember how I reached the boat deck, but somehow I did.
The black smoke was everywhere so intense that no one could
see anything. I was on the port side and simply could see
nothing of what was going on to starboard because of the
flames and smoke. Wherever anyone went he was trapped.'

Morison, in the wheelhouse awaiting instructions, saw the
Captain at the telephone and noted that his face had become
pale and his cheeks sunken.

* * *

Another of the ship's officers caught, as it were, with his pants
down, was the Fifth. This was George Bonwick, who was off
duty and in bed. When he had heard the thump of the bomb
somewhere abaft the officers' quarters, he had neither time nor
need to wonder what it was, or to worry about not having
heard an alarm. Bonwick *knew*. This was something most of
the crew had fearfully half-expected, whilst hoping that it
would never be. He was up, dressed, out and on his way to his
emergency station within two minutes. His job was to muster
and take charge of a fire party on the after square of 'B' deck by
the squash courts.

His cabin was at the after end of the officers' flat on the
starboard side and his quickest way down was via the starboard
companion to the lounge deck and along the Mall. But the
smoke was thick enough to blank out the stairway completely
and, adding to the difficulty, a deckhead had been blown down.

His impression was that the bomb had hit the starboard side,
so looking for a safer route he crossed via the officers' passage
to the port side stairway and so to the Mall. Then the roar of
four massive aircraft engines crescendoed over him and
another attack was on. He flung himself prone and waited for
the blast. When it came it was not loud at all, and seemed to
come from a distance. There was no concussion. The fact was
that the second attack had missed the target completely, as we
have already seen.

Near the revolving door between the Mall and the promenade, Bonwick came across two badly wounded soldiers. They

were right in his path, where he thought someone had dragged them for safety. He stepped over them and went on, his first duty, he considered, being at 'B' deck square. The lights on the main stairway had gone and in the dark he stumbled into a stretcher party on its way down to the sick bay. Bonwick decided to guide them down, borrowing a torch from a Chief Petty Officer who was standing nearby.

Later, at his fire station he found five of his men assembled. There should have been ten, but it was better than none at all; the others might be dead or wounded, and there was nothing he could do to help them. In any case, the fires were not going to wait for the full complement. The eager Bonwick led his men along the alleyway to the main stairs with the idea of getting to the seat of the fires. On the stairway between 'B' and 'A' decks he met the Second Officer, Mr Stanley. Stanley directed him to the fire in the Mayfair Lounge.

Now someone was shouting that the plane was coming back. Bonwick rushed his men, together with some passengers, down the stairs again, this time to the shelter of 'C' deck where he ordered everyone to lie down. The time would have been about 0950.

* * *

Petty Officer George Hitchener had been quietly enjoying a haircut in the barber's shop on 'B' deck. Vaguely he was wondering who on earth in wartime would buy all the junk— the dolls, flags, Chinese boxes, masks, films, cameras and jewelry with which contract ships' barbers load up their shops. There they all were—as plentiful now in the middle of this war as they had been in peacetime, and the barber was no doubt deeply concerned as to how he was going to get his money back.

The Mayfair Lounge was directly above his head, two decks up. The blast of what later came to be known as 'Jope's whopper' ('Yopper's whopper') thumped onto his head like a tent mallet. He too had no doubts about what had happened, and just in case there was room for doubt, the barber's shop roof fell on top of him. Hitchener ripped the cloth away from his neck and was on his way. He was not quite sure where he was supposed to be at times like this, but in any event he went aft.

Things happened so fast that afterwards he could neither remember getting out into the passage nor how he met the little girl whose hand he was holding. All he knew was that suddenly she was there, screaming for her mum. He was very glad when he reached the squash courts opposite the after stair and found Chief Commandant Chitty of the ATS there. This lady was as scared and worried as everyone else, and as uncertain what to do. But when Hitchener gratefully handed the little girl over to her, she was relieved because it gave her something to do and someone to reassure. When Hitchener left them, the ATS Commandant was smiling cheerfully and patting the child's head as it rested in her midriff.

Hitchener was able to climb the stairs (presumably the after stairway), kick through some debris, go to the promenade deck and thence to the orderly room. This was already blazing. He met Garrett there organizing his men and supervizing the laying out and connection of hoses. Garrett told him to take charge while he went below to find out what was wrong with the pumping system. Garrett disappeared forward towards the main stairway entrance.

Hitchener entered the lobby of the Mayfair Lounge. Beneath a pile of debris someone was calling for help. He made his way through the smoke, pulled the debris aside and found a woman there. She was seriously injured and the flames were very near her. He was appalled to see that both her arms had ugly twists in them and he knew they were broken.

He pulled this poor woman out gently by her feet and somehow got her through the revolving doors to the port side promenade. She whispered that her husband was somewhere with her. He lowered her to the deck, making her as comfortable as possible. Getting back into the lobby again was easier said than done. But he tried, desperately hoping he would find the girl's husband. Like Fourth Officer Howell in a similar situation, he could not make it. Fumes, smoke, flames and debris combined to frustrate his efforts. If there *was* anyone in the lounge, there was no way of getting him out, and Hitchener desperately hoped that the man had been killed by the explosion. It would have been more merciful than burning.

He backed out through the mess to the promenade looking for the woman and hoping to be able to take her to a safer place. But, also like Howell, he could not even see her through the blinding smoke. Reluctant to just leave her, if she were still there (someone may have found her and taken her away), he groped forward and found himself at the bottom of the companion leading to the boat deck. Surely there had to be some way out of this holocaust.

★ ★ ★

Petty Officer Thomas Coward was also a member of the naval draft with no special duties. Like Ransome he was filling in his time doing odd jobs in the orderly room. It was a doddle, really, to use a services expression of those times. He had been leaning over the rail with CPO Jevans for some quarter of an hour before Jevans had departed aft to supervise the cleaning of the guns. The mental link with Jevans was probably why the sound of guns firing did not immediately disturb him. But brief seconds later, when the blast of the bomb came, it was out of the blue, and it flung him sideways. A lady and a soldier rushed past him, making for the shelter of the entrance lobby between the orderly room and the Mayfair Lounge. He went with them only to find the place a pandemonium of billowing smoke, screaming women and blazing debris. It was pointless to enter so he made his way to the after stairway back along the promenade and went below to 'C' deck.

Here he met a Petty Officer Reed outside the sick bay. Reed had his arm in a sling. He was uncomfortable, and apprehensive, for he had no lifebelt. If the worse was to happen and he had to swim, he would not have much hope with only one working arm.

Coward hunted around and in a neighbouring cabin found a Board of Trade-type kapok lifejacket. He slipped it over Reed's head, pulled the cords tight and tied them below his chest. He made Reed sit down on the deck telling him to stay there until further orders came.

The nearby sick bay was crowded. Only the doctor and his assistants seemed fully to understand the situation and know what to do. One of these assistants, a Mr Castle, whose real job was second class head steward, was trying to keep the passengers in the alleyway in order, answering questions if he could and pretending to if he could not, and assuring everyone that there was absolutely nothing to worry about. People like Castles are living wonders, able to dispel fear and to calm anxiety under the worst circumstances. Still, it was doubtful if anyone was really convinced, although it was nice to think that they were.

The reality, of course, was that the air was thick with smoke, many people had been hurt or killed, and the continuing screams from forward did nothing to improve matters. The injured, the shocked and the frightened were coming in all the time, and for some minutes Coward helped keep the passageway clear for them and for stretchers.

At some time Castles, also trying to clear the passage, ordered a number of people down to the second class dining room on the deck below. They were better off there anyway, freer from the smoke and the danger of immediate fire. At this time the last bombs had not fallen and Ransome and Garrett had not yet arrived. Petty Officer Reed was where Coward had put him. He had little option, for it was difficult to get up with only one working arm. But he could not help thinking that he would have been better off on an open deck if the ship was abandoned.

Coward climbed the after stairway to 'A' deck and made for his cabin where he hoped to find a torch. His cabin was No 176. Only yards away other cabins were burning fiercely and his own was barely approachable and would be gone in minutes. That is how the whole ship burned—quickly, fiercely, triumphantly, unstoppable. Nevertheless, Coward got his torch and escaped back to 'C' deck. Castles had returned and between them they ran out hoses. When they turned the hydrant wheel barely a trickle of water came through.

* * *

At about 0935 CPO Burley was peering down into the *Salle Jacques Cartier* from 'C' deck. There was a certain amount of smoke down there, but at that stage nothing appeared to be burning. He went forward to the main stairs where a group of people were lying on the floor. But Burley, with unpleasant things happening all about him, was not prepared to join them—although regulations stated that he should do so. He called for volunteers to go with him to see if anything could be done in the burning areas above. Three soldiers and a steward followed him, but they could not get up the stairs. They retreated along 'C' deck to the after stairway which was still fairly clear, climbed to the promenade level and went outside

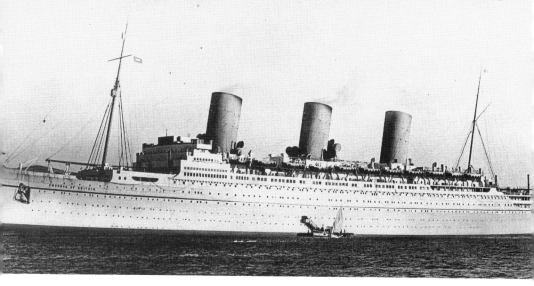

Above Empress of Britain *on her departure from Southampton for her first voyage in 1931.* (Canadian Pacific)

Right *Captain C. H. Sapsworth CVO, Master of* Empress of Britain. (CP Rail Corporate Archives)

Below Empress of Britain *in Quebec before the war.* (George Bonwick)

Left *Oberleutnant Bernard Jope, Commander of the Condor which bombed* Empress of Britain. (Bernard Jope)

Below *Pre-war civil version of the FW Condor.* (Lufthansa)

Right *A painting of the action by the author.*

Middle right *Wartime version of the Condor — the FW 200C.* (Jane's All The World's Aircraft)

Bottom right *Photograph taken by the attacking plane showing a bomb dropping astern.* (Seanews)

Bottom far right *Another photograph taken from the Condor showing the massive clouds of black smoke overlaying the* Empress *within minutes of the attack.* (Seanews)

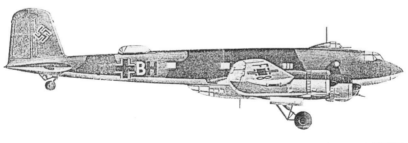

Above *A survivor's view of the* Empress of Britain, *still burning.* (Lady Wendy Lycett and Cdr F. Warrington-Strong)

Below *A rescuing trawler arrives on the scene; the* Empress *burns on.* (Lady Wendy Lycett and Cdr F. Warrington-Strong)

Above *Survivors in a lifeboat approach HMS* Echo. (Lady Wendy Lycett and Cdr F. Warrington-Strong)

Below *The other rescuing warship, HMS* Burza, *in the Clyde after the action.* (Lady Wendy Lycett and Cdr F. Warrington-Strong)

Above *HMS* Echo *approaching the* Empress; *a photograph taken from the port side, amidships.* (Lady Wendy Lycett and Cdr F. Warrington-Strong)

Left *Captain S. H. K. Spurgeon, DSO RAN Ret'd, Commander of HMS* Echo *and seen here in London in 1941 at the time of his investiture.* (Mr Haddon Spurgeon)

Below left *Hans Jenisch, Commander of U32, in 1939 or '40.*

Bottom Empress of Britain *under tow by HM Tugs* Marauder *and* Thames. *(Seanews)*

Above right *Mrs Rona Trotter (left) and Lady Nancye Yarborough at Gourock after the rescue.* (Lady Wendy Lycett)

Right *A newspaper report listing some of the casualties.* (Lady Wendy Lycett)

Far right *Miss and Mr Willis wrapped in blankets after coming ashore. (The Glasgow Herald)*

Sunk Liner Casualties

Chief Officer H. Davies, of the 12,000-tons Canadian Pacific liner Empress of Britain, is now in hospital suffering from machine-gun bullet wounds and other injuries.

This was revealed in the casualty list issued by the company yesterday. The liner sank after being bombed and set on fire in the Atlantic. Chief Officer Davies lives at Great Meols, Cheshire.

Chief Engineer E. Redmond, whose home is at Wallasey, Cheshire, is among the missing. The list also includes:—

DEAD

S. Miller, Strkpr; J. Allen, Asst. Strkpr; A. Curness, Sec. Strkpr; A. Till, Wtr.; A. Powell, Ldry. Boy; J. Watts, Wareh'se Man.; J. Wilkin, Ldry. Boy

MISSING

S. Bradley, Jnr. 4th Engr.; C. Lines, Jun. 10th Engr.; J. England, Engr's Writer; W. Weston, 2nd Bar-kpr.; C. Moreton, 3rd Bar-kpr; M. Ray, 3rd Bar-kpr.; A. Atkinson, Barber; N. Reading, Lnge. Stwd.; J. Allen, Wtr.; J. Ainsworth, Wtr.; D. Britton, 4th Bkr.; J. McPherson, Asst. Btchr.; J. Roberts, Ord. Smn.; M. Mackrell, Boiler Attd.; A. Jeames, Boiler Attd.; A. Knight, Grsr.; A. Russel, Grsr.

IN HOSPITAL

S. Keay, 1st. Offcr.; G. Potts, 2nd Radio Offcr.; H. Arnold, Strkpr.; L. Casswill, Wtr.; E. Meyer., Wtr.; P. Beck, Ldry. Frmn.; K. Fielder, Ldry. Boy; J. Delaney, Ldry. Boy

Left *Dr Edmund Delorme with fellow officers and 'Spot', the troops' terrier mascot, on the bridge of* Empress of Britain *in Cape Town on the outward leg of the final voyage.* (Dr E. Delorme)

Below *(Left to right) Hans Jenisch, Commander of* U32, *George Bonwick, Fifth Officer aboard* Empress of Britain, *and Bernard Jope, pilot of the attacking Condor, meet again in 1981.* (George Bonwick)

and forward towards the first class entrance. Here they were confronted with a massive eruption of fire and smoke from the windows of the Mayfair Lounge and the orderly room.

They unrolled a canvas hose from a firebox, and from somewhere the steward produced a rubber hose. They ran both out, the steward handling the rubber hose and Burley the other. Both were directed towards the inferno in the orderly room, but little water came through.

Then came the roar of the enemy plane overhead, this time from forward. Burley heard the clatter of cannon shot striking along the entire length of the deck above and fell prone. The bomb struck somewhere aft.

Burley lost all sense of time. It seemed to him that immediately after the blast the ship's whistle sounded, finishing with the significant continuous boom. It was time to go to his boat station.

By now the fire had spread across the promenade forward of them from the windows to the rail. The heat was implacable, unavoidable, utterly cruel. Pitch was bubbling in the seams. Burley and the steward took advantage of what water there was, turning their respective hoses on to one another before squeezing their way back to the after stairway, for it seemed the only way out was to go aft. However, smashed and burning boats were hanging from the boat deck, scattering burning debris about the deck. The passage through was impracticable, and the only way now seemed to be to jump overboard and swim to anything they found floating.

Fate intervened. Somehow fate always does, if one may put it like that, for fortuitously a lifeboat came down from the boat deck to stop at the promenade deck near Burley and his companions. They scrambled through a promenade window and went aboard.

This boat had been lowered by the trapped midship gunners who, with some merchant seamen, then slid down into it by the rope and fall cables. They were followed by Mr Keay, the First Officer.

It is difficult to say where Mr Keay came from. The last seen of him was on his return to the bridge after leaving Howell. All that can be said—for Stanley Keay has passed on and cannot tell us—is that on evacuating the bridge with the senior officers, somewhere between the officers' flat, his arrival on the boat deck and his slide down into Burley's boat on the promenade deck, apparently he had broken his arm.

Or that is what Dr Delorme was to think later when he came across the disabled First Officer bravely trying to ignore his injury. For Keay was a brave, uncomplaining man and he kept his wound to himself for nearly 24 hours before seeking help from his friend the ship's doctor. He was to suffer for his fortitude for the rest of his life, with a paralysed arm.

Above them, surrounded by smoke and with flames virtually at his feet, the winchman shouted, 'For Christ's sake get a move on! Me backside's burning off!'

Burley ordered him to let go of the brake and down they went into the water. Last to come down was the winchman to whom willing hands were lent in vigorously putting out the sparks and burns on his trousers. At that time Burley thought that the ship was still moving at about 6 knots.

It was unfortunate that astern of them a motor-boat had also been lowered and was being towed by its rope. When Burley's boat entered the water and the strain was taken on his boat rope it parted, already partly burned through. It was difficult to avoid what followed.

They drifted quickly astern out of control and collided broadside on to the stem of the motor-boat.

* * *

Back aft on the docking bridge, Hipwell, after the first attack, was doing his job bringing up ammunition from the lockers on 'A' deck. They had already fired 43 rounds and the two Hipwell was now bringing up were the last. As it turned out they were useless because they had no fuses.

Hipwell was about to climb the parapet as Jope made his last run in. He heard the roar of the plane, this time from forward, for as we know Jope had decided he would get a better target that way and he had not wanted to waste the last of his bombs.

Hipwell thought that two bombs were dropped, one which hit the sun deck, destroying the 3-inch gun on the docking bridge, and the other striking near the 6-inch gun, failing to explode and rolling into the sea. He actually ascribes these bombs to the second attack, but taken into consideration with other accounts, Hipwell appears to have got a little mixed up. It does not appear that a bomb hit the sun deck during the second attack, although this does not mean that one did not do so. A lot of people involved in the tragedy were naturally a little confused as to what happened when and where. But we shall see.

AB Pullen had also seen the bomber coming and, being without ammunition, he just ducked. The next he knew was the thumping chaos as the blast of the huge bomb smashed the docking bridge and blew the gun apart. Pullen was lucky to survive what was almost a direct hit. Petch and Webb were knocked temporarily unconscious.

At this time Lieutenant-Commander Baker was in the after lounge on 'B' deck. The explosion of the last bomb had been very near and almost overhead and he and his companions were deafened. Adding to the nightmare the lights went out, and they had to grope their way through to daylight, the stewards leading the way to the screen deck.

Here they were to hear the continuous boom of the ship's whistle signalling 'Abandon Ship'. Baker found a small stairway on the port side of the screen deck which took him to 'A' deck. From there he climbed to the promenade. He found the wreck of the gun and the shattered docking bridge. AB Petch was staggering towards the rail, still barely conscious. When Baker grabbed his arm and asked if he was hurt, Petch could not at first reply. Baker made him sit down, his head between his knees. In a nearby locker he found a kapok lifebelt which he slipped over Petch's head, then helped him tie the strings.

There was now some movement on the boats on the starboard side. Between these boats and Baker the deck was burning around a gaping hole. The body of a dead woman lay there, a tennis racket twisted under her torso. This was probably Mrs Wallace, the lady who had left Joan Stephenson at the breakfast table with the promise that they would shortly meet to play tennis. There was nothing Baker could do for her. He dodged around the fire and went to help the men with the boat.

The starboard motor-boat had been swung out from the rail and a seaman was trying to knock off the forward griping line. Baker jumped into the boat to help him. By this time it was about 1010.

* * *

Meanwhile, at about 0940 Mr Moss was still mustering passengers on 'D' deck outside the first class dining saloon, trying to persuade them that there was nothing to be afraid of and that the best thing they could do was to lie down and wait in comfort on the carpets. 'Abandon Ship' had not yet been signalled, as far as he knew, but like others he could not be sure of the sequence and timing of events. Understandably there was fear and confusion all about him and he was just doing his best to handle it.

There were about nine ladies and some men with Moss, and despite his assurances what they wanted to do was to quit this potential underwater tomb and get to what they imagined would be the clear air and greater safety of the boat deck. They would have been disappointed—for if there was anything about the boat deck at this stage, it certainly was not clear air and safety.

With the passages and stairs blocked, quite apart from the lights being out, Moss knew that these people would not have much chance of finding their way upwards themselves. He decided to lead them despite the duties worrying him below.

To those who followed him the journey was simply labyrinthian. He took them aft past the boiler hatch on one side and the *Salle Montcalm* on the other, through the *Jacques Cartier*, up a staircase and through a serving passage and thence to the after dining room. Thence this string of bewildered refugees were taken up the tourist stairway (*terra incognita* to the first class passengers) to the after lounge, also a tourist class area and therefore unknown to them. Confused or not, many of these passengers later ascribed the saving of their lives to Moss and his intimate knowledge of the backways and byways of the ship's interior. But of course Moss was, if one may so express it aboard a ship, on familiar ground.

At one stage Moss met up with Bonwick's fire-fighters and swung his party round them because water was flooding about their feet. On the capstan deck at last, he decided that his charges were as safe as they could hope to be and he left them there in the charge of his writer, Mr Rowe.

Amongst the ladies in this party was Mrs Joan Stephenson. It did not occur to her that Mrs Wallace, with whom she was to have played tennis at this time, may have been killed, and wondered where she had got to.

Moss's next duty was to return below to check as far as he

could, that the lower decks were clear of passengers. He hoped also to find some of the stewards and check with them the matter of the firedoors and watertight doors. He still did not know that by this time 'Abandon Ship' had been signalled, that the bridge was burning or that the Captain himself was struggling to reach a boat.

For ten minutes or more he tried to get back down the way he had come but by now it was impossible. Neither could he get forward. He did the one thing still open to him and this was to return to the capstan deck where he had left his party.

All this had taken time and when he got back to the capstan deck he found that some of his ladies had already departed for the boat deck with Mr Rowe, presumably by the tourist stairway as far as 'A' deck and then by outside companionways and ladders. However, some of them, fancying that the plane might attack again, had preferred to wait in the shelter of the after 'B' deck, that is, the capstan deck. From time to time they were joined by others.

0950: Abandon ship

The Captain was still on his bridge with the Commodore and some of the executive officers; these included Mr Morison and Mr Davies. Morison was standing by in the wheelhouse with the ratings Cluett, Adlam and the quartermasters.

The gunners on the bridge wings fired steadily at the approaching plane which was now attacking from ahead. Sapsworth had been concerned to keep his ship in a position relative to the plane which would give the 3-inch gun a chance to keep it on target, but now with it bearing down from ahead it was not possible and only the Lewis guns on the bridge could fire. The Captain tried to correct the position by circling to port but obviously a plane coming in at 180 miles per hour could not be out-manoeuvred by a ship travelling at 24 knots.

The move to port turned the ship towards the north-west and it was the last move the Captain was to make on the wheel, steadying her up on it. The wind was now firmly on his starboard quarter.

They all ducked as the cannon shells belted into the bridge

and forward superstructure, smashing, among other equipment, the telegraph and wounding the Chief Officer. The
bridge guns were still firing. Those abaft the bridge on the boat
deck amidships could do nothing without the risk of hitting
the bridge. But somewhere, someone with a Lewis gun in those
brief moments scored a hit on one of the plane's engines and
severely damaged it.

The Commodore and Captain saw two bombs leave the
plane and they expected all hell to be let loose. To the Captain
it all seemed very unfair, for there was nothing he could do.
The frightening whine and thump passed overhead as the
bombs disappeared abaft the funnels where they appeared to
impact with massive force and concussion. But, in fact, as we
have seen, one of the bombs did not explode at all. It hit the
deck near the 6-inch gun, made a huge dent in the steel deck
and rolled over the side.

The other *did* explode and, again as we have seen, it did an
awful lot of damage, destroying the 3-inch gun, wrecking boats
and winches, setting fire to others, shattering the docking
bridge, and smashing holes in the tennis court. There were a
number of casualties.

It was at about this time that the engine room became
untenable. Things down there were very bad and getting worse
by the minute with the engineers doing their best to cope,
hampered as they were by their gas-masks.

Generally it was becoming impossible to take any action
which might save the ship. Fires were burning and spreading
freely, communications were out, boats were smashed or
burning, and the fire-fighting capability was practically nil.
The bridge itself was choked with smoke and there was more
than a hint that under the Captain's feet, the officers' quarters
and his own suite were on fire. It was obvious that the Captain
did not have much more time. If he delayed the dreadful,
unthinkable last resort much longer . . .

Then someone telephoned from the engine room. It was the
last telephone call to get through. Sapsworth made up his
mind. For a moment he seemed to mumble into the mouth-
piece. Then, as though the words were forcing their way out,
he said, abruptly, simply: 'Nothing we can do. Stop engines . . .
Abandon the engine room and get to your boats'. Then, looking
about his bridge, he added: 'That's it, Mr Davies. Abandon ship
. . . Passengers must get to their boats.'

Davies was stunned, but he knew that there was no other way. As to the boats . . .

'The boats are burning, Sir.'

'We must do what we can. Abandon ship.'

The siren sounded its six blasts followed by the significant continuing roar.

* * *

The bridge lookouts Cluett, Newstead, Tewry and Adlam heard someone shout the order to abandon. They did not know who it was because everything was obscured by smoke. But the booming siren was authority enough and Cluett said 'Right, lads . . .', and if anyone can think of a more succinct or more Royal Navy way of saying 'Okay! Get on your bikes!', the author would like to hear it.

The ratings, including the gunners, went together, but the officers remained there for some minutes. The ladder which should have taken them to the boat deck was under threat from the flame-tinged smoke and appeared impassable. The men had no alternative but to go forward, that is over and down the bridge superstructure on the side away from the flames, past the cinema operating room, down what remained of the ladder to the forward promenade deck, thence to the forewelldeck with its clusters of bollards, hoists and No 1 hatch, at last to reach the forecastle. The forecastle head at that time was clear of smoke because the wind was coming from starboard. It seemed a good place to sit down and await events. The only trouble was that ships do not keep their lifeboats on their forecastles, and it was a long way down from the head to the sea.

There were already some 60 people there who had by various means escaped the midships holocaust. Others were arriving, some in groups, some singly. Most appeared relieved and confident that they had escaped the major dangers. What they did not know was that they were on one of the most hazardous parts of the ship, not only because of the absence of lifeboats (there were five rafts), and no means of getting to one, but also because beneath them in No 1 hold were 350 tons of sugar which, once the fire got to it, would blaze like pitch. Neither did they know that within a very short time as the wind shifted, they were to be engulfed in blinding smoke, or that the boats which should have come to their rescue, through a number of mischances, culpabilities, even perhaps neglect and mismanagement, would not reach them.

* * *

At the sounding of 'Abandon Ship', Mr Morison was told to get to the lifeboats in his charge, Nos 6 and 8 on the port side. He made what was in itself a hazardous journey to the boat deck— a hasty scramble down the already burning companion abaft the officers' quarters and a scrape along a portion of blazing deck. Here he met the Second Officer Mr Stanley. Stanley had heard the 'Abandon Ship' and had quit his fire-fighting on the promenade to climb to the boat deck where his two boats were. He found a raging fire there, with the deck and boats abaft No 8 ablaze and unapproachable. They were soon joined by the wounded Chief Officer who under the Captain's orders had left the bridge shortly after Morison. The three officers discussed the paramount importance of getting away quickly such boats as remained intact.

* * *

Bernard Jope in his Condor had had enough. He had also *done* enough, for it was obvious that his massive target was burning out of control and would be abandoned. He radioed his base to this effect and decided that it was time to go home.

Although today there is a certain histrionic hint of concern for loss of life in his comments, and incidentally resentment at the suggestion of deception in his attack, his immediate regret was that all his bombs had not done the job for which they were intended. One dreads to think of what would have happened to the *Empress* and her passengers if they had. A 550-lb bomb is a big bomb, capable on land of destroying a block of buildings. On a ship even one such explosion, as foregoing events have shown, was devastating and had all the bombs done their job it is improbable that anyone would have survived. But that is the nature of war—and *man* at war.

Jope switched off his damaged engine and cruised off to the south and the refuge of Brest before British planes arrived to hit the hitter. In the event, the first British plane, a Royal Navy Skua, did not arrive until half an hour after Jope had gone. It is difficult to see what a Navy dive-bomber could have done to help the *Empress* but that is the way things go. It might just have been looking for a Condor to shoot down.

* * *

Down in the engine room, Junior Second Engineer Evans still had no idea where his Chief, Mr Redmund, was. He did not know that Redmund had tried to get below but because of the fires in the engineers' passage on 'B' deck had been unable to do so. He had gone aft where he met Bonwick, helping him to organize his men and equipment.

Evans got the message to abandon the engine room and get to the boats from an assistant. He simply had no idea what had happened except that this ship which had been so beautiful, safe and glamorous only half an hour before, must now be burning beyond control. He snapped his orders to the stunned men about him. Abandon the *Empress of Britain*? Just like that? And only half an hour before . . .

Everything that had to be done was done with a desperate efficiency in an atmosphere becoming increasingly airless; by now they could hardly breathe. The fuel oil to the pumps was shut off, machinery shut down, switches thrown. There was not much time. They did their job and Evans gave the order to evacuate. They set about getting away and up out of this smoke-ridden hell which could so easily become their tomb. Evans himself barely remembers climbing the labyrinth of steel ladders and gratings, but somehow he reached the tourist stairway. On 'D' deck he found water flooding the alleyways and he thought that it must have come from fractured mains. There was little light on 'B' deck and he could not get to his cabin on the starboard side alleyway. He went via the port side passage to the shelter deck and thence to the capstan deck which was about as far aft as he could go and where he found a number of engineers, amongst them Mr Redmund. Evans greeted him a little tersely. No doubt he would not have done so had he known the difficulties which had confronted the Chief in trying to get down to the engine room—although Evans and his men had managed to get *up*. Further, poor, paunchy, brave Jimmy England, whose story was revealed later by Dr Delorme, had gone up and down not once but six times. Unhappily—for hindsight and mischievous comment can be cruel—Redmund never did get the opportunity to tell his story. Within half an hour he had disappeared and was never seen again.

Evans explained to Redmund what had happened below and that to the best of his knowledge everything which had to be done had been done. There was some half-hearted discussion about the possibility of going down again to look at the pumps, but they had closed down when the electricity supply was cut off and it was really quite pointless. In any case, Evans was sure that the real fault had been fractured mains. The flooding lower decks were a clear indication.

* * *

In the operating theatre the electricity had ceased and for some time smoke had been pouring in through the ventilator ducts. Men were choking, not the least of them Dr Delorme and his assistants. It was rapidly becoming an impossible situation and a tragic one too, for those men were working to save lives in that deep grey gloom.

They overcame some of the problem by stuffing clothing into the ducts. They also rigged up some emergency lighting with auxiliary lamps and so carried on their desperate work.

The operating room had not escaped damage for the after bulkhead had buckled under the bomb blast. A cabinet full of glassware and instruments had crashed to the deck and what with one thing and another Delorme, being a man of masterly imagination, found himself comparing the dismal scene to the orlop deck of the *Victory* as Nelson lay dying.

Two tragic and heroic events have stuck in Delorme's mind ever since the loss of the *Empress*. One concerns the magnificent work done by the engineer's writer, one Jimmy England. He was middle-aged, plump and short but veritably a David in courage. He came staggering into the sick bay bearing an injured stoker on his back. He had carried him from 'G' deck up four levels, through innumerable passages and alleyways, up steel ladders and over steel gratings, dodging smoke and fire until he got his man to the sick bay. And having done all that he had soaked his handkerchief with water, tied it around his mouth and off he had gone again. Ten minutes later Jimmy turned up with another injured man who, but for Jimmy, would have died an isolated and nasty death. But that was not the end of it, for having made this delivery Jimmy went off again and returned with yet another man he had rescued from death.

Each time he came into the sick bay Delorme spoke to him telling him he had done enough, trying to persuade him not to go down again. But five times he went down and five times he came back, each time with an injured man. Delorme could not imagine how he did it, how he had weaved his way through burning and sometimes flooding alleyways, up and down steel ladders and stairways, avoiding flames when he came to them and finding alternative routes. The only person who knew was the magnificent Jimmy himself.

Jimmy England did not return from his sixth journey. Presumably he died, choking and burning in some tiny alleyway or at the bottom of some red-hot steel ladder.

Later in the war the disappearance and death of Jimmy England worried Delorme and he tried to get some recognition for this unsung hero. His enquiries were ignored. He has often wondered why. One reason, he thought, was that whilst he knew the man as 'Jimmy England', he could not afterwards be sure that this truly apt name was not a nickname, and as such would not have appeared on crew lists. The author himself made enquiries and discovered that Jimmy England really was Jimmy England and that he had been one of the longest-serving members of the crew, serving on and continuously after the first voyage in 1931. He was a native of Shirley, Southampton.

In view of the recommendations made for awards as a result of the action one wonders upon what criteria such recommendations are made when Jimmy and several others, showing great devotion to duty and the staunchest behaviour, were left out. Dr Delorme was not able to pursue his enquiries. If he had done so successfully, Jimmy might have become one of the very early posthumous George Medallists.

Shortly after the arrival of the bomb which destroyed the 3-inch gun, Dr Delorme was called to the port side laundry. A young laundry boy had been buried in the debris and was hopelessly trapped. There seemed no way of getting him out and with flames only yards away the horror of the situation may be imagined.

Delorme did not know whether to pray for the boy or to take the drastic action he did take a few moments later. He explained the desperate situation to the boy, telling him the only way to get him out was to amputate his arm at the elbow. The boy was near collapse but still managed to whisper, 'You get me out of here . . .'

But there was more trouble. It was impossible to use a general anaesthetic—gas, in other words—because of the nearby flames. Again Delorme explained. Again the boy nodded.

'Just you get me out of this . . .'

The doctor performed the operation with a mild local anaesthetic—it was successful, and the boy survived. One wonders where he is today and one also wonders who was under the greater stress and, indeed, who was the greater hero. In any event, neither the boy nor Delorme received even a 'Mention' in the awards.

* * *

After leaving his own room, where through the porthole he had seen the attacking aircraft at a distance spraying the ship with cannon fire, Mr Pearch had joined his Deputy Purser, two assistant pursers and a writer in the bureau and assisted them in placing cash, documents and valuables into canvas bags. They were still in the bureau when the final attack came. Like others, they did not hear the 'Abandon Ship' signal which followed.

Having ensured that all the valuables had been collected, Pearch now had to get to his muster station. Knowing by his previous efforts that it would be hopeless to mount the main stairway, he instructed his staff and some others (who, in the vague belief that if anyone ought to know what he was doing it would be the Purser, had gathered around the bureau) to follow him along 'B' deck starboard alleyway. It was in darkness but by holding hands they were able to grope their way through the ship's staff quarters to the light and air space below the forward lounge. This was a third class recreation area abaft the forewelldeck.

They found there the third class head steward, Mr Metcalfe, with some ship's personnel and some RN ratings, all of them, like Pearch, wondering now that they had achieved some apparent element of safety in the forward part of the ship, how on earth they were going to get to their boat stations. As they were to discover, there was no way.

Pearch, noting the build-up of smoke, ordered everyone forward to the forecastle. There were already a considerable number of people there, the less sanguine among them perhaps wondering, if the smoke persisted, where they could go from there. The long, long drop into the sea seemed the only answer.

But, as it happened, the ship, which had veered off almost in a north-westerly direction, with the smoke billowing from her after parts to smother the parts forward of the bridge, now moved round towards the north-east and shifted the smoke away. Now they could see behind them clearly. One of the things they saw was the blazing navigation bridge and beneath it the blackened ruin of what had been the officers' quarters. It was a horrifying promise of what was to come.

Pearch noted that there were a number of wounded and otherwise hurt passengers. He also noted that there was no first aid equipment. Since, as it turned out, there was none in the lifeboats either, the question 'Why?' was one asked many times on that tragic day.

Certainly first aid equipment was not Pearch's affair, although from his knowledge of the ship he was pretty sure that there were stretchers and other materials elsewhere than on the forecastle, so he was compelled to wonder why it was necessary for the injured to be carried on planks and broken doors and for bandages to be improvized. The fact was that of course there were stretchers and first aid materials, but tragically they were all concentrated around the sick bay area and nothing had been done to establish casualty stations elsewhere, forward or aft. Something *should* have been done. But *who* should have done it? Dr Delorme? After all, as we have seen, there really were adequate medical personnel on board for the comparatively small complement involved, and they could easily have been organized to establish and man casualty stations. But then again it might be said that the organization of service facilities was the affair of the services themselves. There was an Officer Commanding Troops on board, in charge of all service personnel, male and female, single or married, and of all three services. He was fully equipped with adjutant and staff, and one would have thought that someone amongst them would have had the experience or foresight to insist upon the dispersal of first aid facilities to places other than the sick bay.

It might be pushing it a bit to suggest that perhaps the

ubiquitous Commander Garrett might have looked into it, for he had assumed or been pushed into so much responsibility in other ways that something obvious like the establishment of casualty stations should not have been missed. That is unfair, of course, for truly it was not and could not have been Garrett's responsibility. And in case it may be thought that the author is being over-critical of Garrett, he would like to say now that everything did indeed point to Garrett being a most efficient man. In this respect there follows a quote from a letter written to the author by Mrs Rona Trotter's son, John Trotter, on behalf of his sick mother in 1983:

'Commander Garrett was a very efficient and charming man . . . before the attack he had on several occasions expressed his concern over the lack of proper boat drill. He also complained to the Captain but it would appear with little effect . . . apart from his concern over the lack of boat drill he had been full of gloom about the whole voyage . . .'

A report by a Naval Stores Officer, Mr Willis, later in this book, also bears testimony to the morale-boosting efficiency of Commander Garrett.

Today perhaps it does not much matter if a conclusion is reached that the voyage prior to the tragedy was a bit of a lark, for no one is going to get shot for it. Then again, perhaps it was just another example of the way the British sometimes do things. The events leading up to the kerfuffle in the Falklands is an instance of the British persistence in solemnly lining themselves up for almost certain defeat and then seizing upon events to turn near defeat into victory. And then wondering if the victory was really worth the trouble before setting off once again on a new road to yet another near defeat. British history is full of examples . . .

* * *

George Trotter had left the sick bay at about 0950, shortly before the last bomb destroyed the 3-inch gun. Like others he instinctively tried to get forward to the main stairs but the smoke was so thick and everywhere so dark that he was forced to retreat, and after some hesitation on the after 'A' deck square he eventually came out to the daylight on 'B' deck. Part of the after 'B' deck was a shelter deck, but it was possible from there to see to some extent what was going on astern and forward. It was here that Trotter was to face one of the most unnerving things of all—the periodic explosions from the ammunition lockers on 'A' deck where the 6-inch ammunition was stored. Any single 6-inch shell explosion could send the whole magazine sky high and destroy the entire after parts of the ship.

One other thing worrying Trotter was that in all this time he had not set eyes on a single ship's officer, and he wondered why. It was unfair but understandable. But, in fact, it seems that the Fifth Officer, George Bonwick, must also have been at the after end of 'B' deck for some minutes whilst Trotter was there. At any rate, Trotter was on 'B' deck aft with no idea what to do next. He retreated to the after lounge where he simply waited for something to happen.

Whilst he was there a ship's officer *did* arrive. This was the Chief Steward, Mr Moss, who turned up with his ladies and, listening to their chatter, Trotter realized that they considered their lives had been saved by Mr Moss and his expert knowledge of the ship's interior, for with so many of the known ways blocked by fire and debris, by themselves they would inevitably have been lost in the darkness below.

Bonwick meanwhile had hurriedly gone down to the shelter of 'C' deck square via the after stairway to get away from the latest air attack. When a bomb fell it seemed to him that it was deliberately aimed at him because the blast was immediately over his head. Wreckage fell about him. Momentarily at a loss as to whether to stay in the vicinity and deal with any fires springing up or go to the Mayfair Lounge where he knew there was a huge fire, he tried to get instructions from the bridge. There was a pantry between the after stairway and the hospital which had a telephone. The exchange did not answer.

He decided then to take his party aft together with some passengers who had gathered about him. He reached the after lounge at about 1000. He mustered the passengers and told them to remain there awaiting instructions; he then departed with his men, proceeding up the tourist stairway to 'A' deck where he found a fire raging near the isolation hospital. They ran out their hoses directed the nozzles at the fire and opened the valves. Once more, very little water came out. They unscrewed their hoses and moved to the starboard side, trying again. Still very little water.

Bonwick then recalled that there was a service pipe on both sides of 'B' deck. He led his party down, leaving the nozzle where it was and stretching the hose down the stairs to the service pipe and connecting it up. He opened the valve and the resultant gush offered immediate hope, but then quickly subsided into a bare trickle.

He refused to give up. Puzzled and frustrated, this dogged young officer transferred his efforts to the port side service pipe. Again just a trickle of water came through. Virtually the only chance he had now to fulfil his duty as a fire-fighting officer was to use the extinguishers in each corner of 'B' deck square. He set off but 'B' deck alleyway had become a tunnel of fire.

In the meantime, unbeknown to him 'Abandon Ship' had been signalled. But still all the necessary signs were there, for the fires had assumed devastating proportions and he guessed that there was little hope of putting them out. He thought of going down to 'C' deck to get forward along the alleyway there. Perhaps, he thought, it might even be possible to go forward via 'D' or even 'E' deck where the fires might not yet have got a hold.

But 'C' deck forward of the hospital was already in trouble and Delorme was arranging to evacuate his patients. As for 'D' deck, water was slopping about the passages and in any case both on 'D' and 'E' decks the firedoors and watertight doors had been closed and locked. Below that was the engine room. It was a long way down and although he did not yet know it, it had been abandoned.

So Bonwick did not go forward. It seemed pointless and hazardous to go down. 'A' deck, with its bomb-like magazine, did not invite him upwards. So aft he went between the shelter deck and the capstan deck where he decided to remain.

Now he had his first opportunity to look over the side and it was with surprise that he saw boats in the water, some of them well away from the ship and most of them apparently almost empty. He knew then that no further instructions would come to him because the 'Abandon Ship' signal must have been given whilst he was below and unable to hear.

Bonwick was a very unhappy man. He waited by the rail terribly conscious of the ammunition exploding just one deck up and threatening the entire stern parts of the ship. He hoped someone would see their plight, come in close and take them off. He did not know that whilst he had been below hunting about for water outlets that worked, a boat *had* pulled in and gone away fully loaded.

* * *

Major Trotter was in the after lounge on 'B' deck, wondering what to do next. Up to this time he, like George Bonwick, had not known for sure that the *Empress* was being abandoned. Whilst this might seem surprising, it must be remembered that both these officers had mostly been below decks and at the after end of the ship. The intercom, like the lighting, ventilation and water supply, had broken down and they were by no means alone in not knowing what had happened. Dr Delorme, for example, down on 'C' deck was also, and almost literally, in the dark.

When Trotter heard someone yell that the German plane was coming back he rushed outside to the capstan deck and peered anxiously forward. He came to a knowledgeable conclusion.

'German bomber, my arse!' he said to himself. 'That's an RN Skua!'

Although the sight of a British plane was a relief, he could not help wondering how a naval dive-bomber was going to help. What they really wanted was for some ship's officer to come along and tell them everything was all right or if it was not all right, then for a couple of destroyers and a few flying-boats to arrive.

In fact, a ship's officer did arrive, as we have already seen, in the shape of the Chief Steward with his ladies. He did not tell Trotter that everything was 'all right', because although he had a pretty good idea of what was going to happen, no one had yet officially told him the ship was being abandoned. It was at this stage that they became aware that lifeboats had been lowered, for a hundred yards off their port quarter two boats were drifting by. Below and forward there was another lifeboat with four men in it trying to pull into the side. Everyone began to yell, encouraging the men in their efforts, and when they were close Moss and Trotter threw ropes over and with these the men on the boat held her steady.

The ladies were then instructed to climb down. They would have to move quickly in case the boat got out of hand and drifted away. Furthermore, there was always the fear in Trotter's mind that the exploding ammunition might also get out of hand and blow the stern to glory.

Among these ladies were Joan Stephenson and Lady Yarborough. Trotter took the brief opportunity to ask if they knew what had happened to his sister-in-law, but no one recalled having seen Rona Trotter since the previous evening.

Most of the ladies behaved magnificently and did as they were told. Some were stronger and perhaps more courageous than others. Lady Yarborough, for example, went down without hesitation hand over hand like a gym instructor. So did Joan Stephenson who, as she now says, did not even get her feet wet. Others slipped down and badly skinned their hands. Not all the ladies went. There were still a few optimists who, wary of the 40-foot climb down a rope, were unreasonably of the opinion that it was up to the ship's company to get them to safety without they themselves risking their necks.

It was an odd sort of time for them all—something one might read about in a book or which only happened to other people, many years ago or a long way off.

At the bottom of the rope, Trotter's luck ran out for the boat drifted and he had to enter the water and swim. The worst part of it, he found, was letting go of the rope. The ship was rising and falling anything up to 10 feet and he was being dipped in and out like a teabag. But there it was—a bit of a wild scramble, one last unnerving clutch for the rope and then he was floating up and down like a paper boat on a pond in Hyde Park.

The lifeboat was about 20 yards away and drifting, but a wave sent it crashing back towards the ship's side and he could so easily have been crushed. But the Trotters were survivors, and he escaped. Willing hands fended off and George Trotter, safe and thankful, was hauled aboard looking, as he was later to say to his nephew, John Trotter, Rona Trotter's son, like a tomcat under the hose.

He was exhausted. He flopped down in the bottom of the boat cold, wet and worried. He lay alongside a lady who had injured herself when she let go of the rope too soon, crashed onto a thwart and badly banged her head.

Two seamen took charge, one forward and one aft. He did

not know if they were ship's company or Royal Navy except that they both wore RN issue inflatable lifejackets.

* * *

Rona Trotter was on the promenade deck when one of her companions shouted that the German plane was coming back. This was the second attack and like the first it came from astern. As we know, its bombs missed and disappeared into the sea. But its cannons raked the entire length of the sun deck and bridge, causing many casualties and a great deal of damage. The plane roared over and was gone.

Today she does not remember how long she stayed on the promenade deck and neither does she recall the last attack and the bomb strike aft. But she must have been there for perhaps half an hour because when later she climbed a steel ladder to reach the boat deck, boats were already being lowered. 'Abandon Ship' must have sounded, and that had been shortly after 0950.

On the boat deck, fumes and ash from windward were pouring across the deck, smothering those assembled there. Everyone had difficulty in breathing, but there was little they could do about it for within minutes the fires on the upper decks had become so fierce with the tennis court and sun deck blazing that there simply was nowhere to go. Rona Trotter saw boats damaged and on fire, and beyond the flames, and for her unreachable there was a bustle of sailors trying to lower a boat which presumably had not been damaged. She had the dreadful sense of being trapped.

It is difficult to work out how long she was on the boat deck. Again debatably, perhaps, half an hour or more. The next seen of her she had decided that the only way out was overboard and she was clambering hand over hand down a rope to the sea, with a steward following her. At the bottom of the rope she hesitated—for where was there to go now except into the water? She hung on to that hazardous refuge for about ten minutes, by which time it was probably about 1100 hours.

* * *

Under ideal conditions, if such an expression may reasonably be used for any situation of this nature, the *Empress* would have been allowed to lose way before being abandoned and the lifeboats would not have been lowered until the ship was stationary or moving very slowly. Then, when the boats were put into the water, they would not drift astern or away from the area where survivors might be swimming or from where they might pull into the side of the ship to take off those who were stranded.

In any case, boats would first have been lowered to the promenade or embarkation deck and passengers mustering there could have embarked in an orderly fashion and under discipline. But this was by no means a normal abandoning, if there is such a thing, and the situation was far from ideal. Many boats had been destroyed and others were burning. Others could not be reached because they were cut off by burning decks. Again, it had not been possible for the Captain to order engines to be reversed and so slow down the ship because 'Stop Engines', 'Abandon the Engine Room' and 'Abandon Ship' had, of necessity, been ordered simultaneously. Altogether it was, to quote one expert, 'a fine to-do'.

The 'to-do' was aggravated when boats were lowered directly to the water whilst the ship was still under way—quoted as being anything between 4 and 15 knots—because they were liable to collide, get tangled up in their own and others' boat ropes or get in the way of other boats coming down on top of them. All these things happened. It was in truth a 'fine to-do'.

The Captain was between the devil and the deep with a vengeance. He and the Commodore were the last to leave the bridge. The time must then have been about 1010. The rooms below the navigation bridge including his own suite were a holocaust and the navigation bridge itself was belching great volumes of smoke. For the first time Sapsworth was able to get a more or less positive look at the sea behind him and there he saw some boats floating away almost empty. Perhaps this was inevitable in view of the inability of anyone to communicate or issue orders between forward, amidships and aft. People just had to solve their own problems in their own areas without directions from the bridge.

Sapsworth guessed that many people must have dispersed forward and aft to get away from the holocaust amidships, but he had no idea how many or how they were making out, and he desperately hoped that the boats he saw in the water would somehow get back to them.

Emerging from below the navigation bridge and trying to reach the boat deck, he saw a group of about 40 men on the foredeck, below and forward of the forward promenade deck. They were cut off from access to stairways to the boat deck or forward to the forewelldeck. This must have been just abaft of No 2 hatch which was now belching out smoke and flame. These men were hopelessly trapped. Sapsworth called to them: 'Come along, you men! You may be able to get up this way to the boats.'

But there was fire behind and above them in the Empress Room, and fire before them in the hatch. They shouted that there was no way they could get up or away. The Captain told them to unlash the rafts and throw them overboard and jump after them. It was easier said than done.

The smoke was then so heavy that the Captain could see nothing forward of those unfortunate men and could only guess at the number of people in similar situations. There were indeed people forward on the other side of the billowing smoke, by now some 300 of them crowding onto the forewelldeck, forecastle and forecastle head—300 men, women and children who appeared to have no future but the long drop into a hostile sea. Amongst them were Garrett, Pearch, Adlam, Cluett and Ransome, to name but a few.

Sapsworth and the Commodore climbed through the debris and eventually reached the boat deck where they again met the Chief Officer who, it will be remembered, when told to do what was necessary after 'Abandon Ship' had been signalled, had left the bridge ahead of the others to assist in fire-fighting as best he could, and to help direct the lowering of boats. When the Captain met him now he was trying to handle a fire at the forward end of the boat deck. The Commodore stopped to help him, and in doing so lost touch with the Captain.

To Sapsworth it seemed doubtful that passengers could board their boats on the promenade deck because of the fires blazing at various places along its length. He saw Mr Stanley's two boats (Nos 2 and 4) on the port side hanging at that deck and observed that flames were licking at them through the prom windows. He ordered Stanley and his assistant, Mansell, to lower the boats almost to sea level where they were to wait for way to be lost before entering the water. No 2 went down with some men aboard directly to the water where, naturally enough, with the ship's speed being what it was, she was difficult to handle. Under Stanley's instructions they could not slip. No 4 was taking passengers through a promenade window. She was then lowered to lay just clear of the water.

With the flames now very close, the Captain was trapped on the boat deck with Stanley and Mansell. But seeing men in the sea swimming for their lives, he ordered his two officers to launch rafts over the side from their positions beneath the davits of No 2. They got one raft away, too late to help the men who in the meantime had drifted astern. The second raft remained and burned.

Meanwhile, Nos 6 and 8 had not yet been lowered, and as it happened No 6 could not go down because No 4, having now reached the water, was dragging on its rope directly below it.

* * *

Mr Howell heard 'Abandon Ship' whilst he was still on the promenade. Like Petty Officer Hitchener, he was searching for the injured woman whom he had rescued and placed in some temporary safety. At the signal he went back into the smoke but could not find her. He hoped someone had moved her whilst he was away. He was now torn between going back to the bridge—if he could get there—where he was still officially relieving officer of the watch, or more pragmatically, going directly to his emergency boat station. He chose the latter.

The boats in his charge were on the port side with Morison— Nos 6 and 8. His job was to assist in the lowering and to organize the passengers mustered on the embarkation deck. But, of course, muster stations had gone by the board in most cases because there was either no way of getting to them, the boats themselves were burning or else flames from the promenade windows effectively prevented the boats from stopping at the embarkation deck.

When Howell arrived, Stanley, standing up on the winch of No 2 was slowly releasing the friction brake to allow gravity to take the boat down under control. Mr Mansell had done the same with No 4. It was at this stage that Captain Sapsworth arrived and decided that both boats would have to go down to just above the water level. Howell knocked the gripes away on his own No 6 and climbed to the winch.

All this was taking place on the forward part of the boat deck where a considerable fire was threatening to isolate them.

Howell wanted to get his boat down before the fire got to it, but taking a precautionary look over the side he was appalled to see that No 4, after embarking some passengers halfway down, had now entered the water, was pulling back on its falls and threshing about directly below his boat. Howell yelled at Morison. Morison shouted down to the Petty Officer in the stern of No 4 to get out of the way.

'Slip, man! You're in the way! Get her out of it!'
The Petty Officer was George Hitchener.

* * *

The last we had seen of Hitchener was when he left the prom deck to climb the companion to the boat deck looking for someone to help him move an injured lady. He met the Chief Officer who shook his head impatiently.

'Look, Petty Officer—you aren't the only one in trouble. Never mind about getting your girl friend to the hospital—get her to a boat. You'll just have to handle it yourself.'

The thing was that Chief Officer Davies was not only a man very worried about his ship and his passengers, but he was also in pain. He had been wounded in the chest.

Three naval signalmen were standing by and Hitchener ordered them to go down with him to help find the injured woman. They found her. They had another stroke of luck, too. A boat was being lowered from the deck above. There was only one man in it, a wounded Chief Gunner's Mate, name unknown. The boat stopped at the promenade level. Hitchener and his helpers carried the lady to it and handed her over the gunnel to the wounded man, who did what he could to settle her in the bottom. She was in great pain, barely conscious and still whispering for someone to help her husband. But there was nothing Hitchener could do. If the man survived they would find him ashore—*if* they got ashore themselves.

He stood by waiting for other passengers when suddenly without warning the boat went down quickly and came to rest some feet above the water. But, of course, the sea was not a millpond, and shortly afterwards the boat was in the water dragging on its ropes. It was No 4.

The ship's speed by now could have been anything between 4 and 10 knots—or, according to some sources, 15 knots. No one was sure. But certainly it was too great to slip. Forward of

No 4, No 2 was finding it hard to stay alongside but could not slip because No 4 was directly behind and had to carry on dragging on its falls. Suddenly the boat rope of No 4 carried away, burned through, so that she too was being towed by her fall cables. Hitchener made a grab for a rope hanging from overhead and he and his passengers began pulling back to the ship's side. But again things went wrong. The rope got caught up in the forward thwart and under the dragging pressure the thwart gave way. Again, as one might put it, it was a pretty fine to-do.

But they grabbed yet another rope, this time a ladder, and again pulled No 4 back. Suddenly there were shouts from above and, looking up the immense cliff-like ship's side, Hitchener saw a boat hanging directly above his head. A ship's officer was yelling at him to slip. But that was all very well. He did not have many on board and if he slipped now, the boat would drift astern quickly and be denied to many people who needed it. But at this stage the initiative was taken from him.

* * *

After the bomb hit on the docking bridge, Hipwell had gone aft looking for his mates. To port the ladder had been destroyed, so he crossed to the starboard ladder. He found Pullen and Webb trying to douse a fire and helped them.

Hipwell recalled that there was a hose box just inside the promenade deck on the port side and he and Webb went to look for it. They ran out the hose but it was about ten feet too short to reach the fire area and the trickle of water that came from it was in any case useless.

By this time they were being threatened by a fire on the after prom. They squeezed their way between the contactor house and No 4 hatch to return to the starboard ladder. Beside the contactor house they found AB Andrews. He was very badly wounded.

Andrews was one of the gun crew, and had been stationed in the after wheelhouse to man the telephone. The explosion had flung him across the after promenade where the contactor house had concealed him.

There were now six of them—Petch, who had now recovered, Pullen, Webb, Hipwell, the incapacitated Andrews and one other rating of the guncrew, AB McLean. Then they heard the ammunition exploding below and they realized that it would not be long before the magazine went up. They went for the boats.

Pullen and Webb climbed the ladder, found some rope and with this they hauled Andrews up to the boat deck. Several boats had already been lowered and could be seen drifting astern. The time must have been about 1030.

* * *

The diligent Commander Garrett had returned to the promenade after making a hazardous passage up the practically unscalable main stair. The situation here was frightening, bringing home to him the futility of continuing to fight the fires without adequate means. He had come to the point where the safety of his men had become critical. He had not heard the signal to abandon ship, but the outcome of a combination of uncontrollable fires, failure of the water supply and the huge mass of overhanging smoke was unmistakeable. The ship could not be maintained. He told his men to get to their boat stations.

The quickest way to the boat deck should have been forward to a companionway abreast of the forward funnel. Unhappily, the deck between them and this stairway was an inferno. The orderly room behind them was as bad, so that they appeared to be virtually trapped. However, if they could get back inside to the main stairs and again negotiate its hazards they might still get down to a lower deck not yet impassable and find their way forward along an alleyway.

They made their dangerous entry through the wreck of the first class entrance and groped their way past the shop. Some of them of a stronger heart found their way down the stairs. Others were more timid and did not, and probably died as the price of their faintheartedness.

Two decks down, Captain Black was still with his party awaiting instructions, also unaware that the ship was being abandoned. He was in a state of great anxiety and indecision and Garrett was impatient with him, telling him to use his initiative. He suggested that he take his party down to 'C' deck which, as far as could be seen, although thick with smoke was still not burning. He might be able to disperse his people either forward or aft to some measure of safety either through the hospital area or the crew's quarters.

Black led his party down and went forward following the path of Metcalfe and Ransome. It was an unnerving experience in the darkness, wandering through an unknown part of the ship. Most of them reached the open forward decks and survived.

Garrett himself went forward along 'B' deck, but struck trouble. A fireproof door had, quite properly, been locked. There seemed to be nothing for it but to break it down—far easier said than done. But good luck intervened with the appearance of a steward searching for lost passengers. He unlocked the door and escorted the party through to the airing space forward of the bridge and beneath the forward lounge.

By this time the bridge was blazing. The wind was still on the starboard beam, driving the smoke towards the port side boats. But on the starboard side Garrett saw a number of boats in the water, well away from the ship, and it seemed to him that most of them were empty. He estimated that there were about 300 persons congregated forward of the bridge, many of them men from his own raft, some needing medical attention.

Those boats, he considered (he did not know the full story) must have been lowered in panic by people who had not known how to handle them. And it all showed how right he had been to question the manner in which boat drills had been, or, perhaps more truthfully, had *not* been, carried out during the voyage. Later he learned from Commander Baker that in his opinion the boats, or some of them, had been lowered and slipped whilst the ship was still travelling at about 15 knots. Then his anger knew no bounds. But Baker, too, may have been wrong, although the ship had been travelling at a fairly massive 24 knots when the signal to abandon had gone.

Garrett could not see what was happening astern because of the bridge structure and the curve of the hull. He and his 300 were to all intents and purposes in a world of their own. By 1130 the flames had spread from the bridge downwards across the forward deck, where the Captain had seen the 40 trapped men, and all were threatened.

Garrett was a practical and objective man and it seems probable that he had automatically assumed responsibility for the safety of these people. It was now up to him to do everything he could to ensure that they survived. He began to think in terms of rafts.

* * *

There were already some 2-300 persons massed on the fore-castle area when Chief Petty Officer Ransome arrived—a mixture of all services, ship's crew and civilians, all of them looking out to sea wondering why the boats lying out there were not coming back to take them off.

It was Ransome who, under Garrett's instructions, gathered his men and set them to making rafts. As Garrett had noted, there were already several properly constructed rafts lashed to the decks, made from bulky lengths of timber firmly fixed to sealed 40-gallon drums above and below and surrounded by looped lifelines. But they both knew that if it came to the crunch, there would not be enough.

They set about the task with customary Royal Navy zeal, using anything that would float. They knocked out wedges to get at hatch covers, pulled down blackout screens, unscrewed awning spars. They lashed wooden gratings and ladders together and unlashed wash deck and lifebelt lockers. They cut lines from buoys, lashed mooring hawsers together and in the end had as motley a collection of potential lifesaving devices as one could ever hope to see.

By this time the bridge structure was burning freely from the forward promenade deck to the compass platform. The forewelldeck was smoke-ridden and passengers had mostly forsaken it for the clearer air of the forecastle and forecastle head. But as the wind gusted and the smoke momentarily cleared, high up, slung out from the starboard side of the boat deck, a solitary lifeboat could be seen. It appeared to be undamaged. Just possibly it could be reached.

Garrett discussed it with Ransome. To reach it would be a momentous and dangerous task, if indeed it was reachable at all. It would mean penetrating back across the forewelldeck, across the burning foredeck to the already burning area which at better times had been used for a canvas swimming bath for third class passengers and in which No 2 hatch was shooting up billows of smoke, and then somehow contriving to climb either to the forward promenade or through the officers' quarters to the boat deck. Neither Garrett nor Ransome knew that the latter had been negotiated only with the greatest difficulty by the Captain and Commodore, and as for the foredeck it was the place where Sapsworth had seen the 40 trapped men and heaven only knows what had happened to them. It seemed a hopeless task—a sort of 'Mission Impossible'. But they had a go.

Ransome borrowed a gas-mask from a lady. Garrett wore his own. Altogether 20 men set off on this expedition. Somehow they did cross the foredeck and by one means or another a few of them climbed the cliff-like structure of the bridge, probably using the remains of the stairway which at better times had led from the officers' quarters to the first class promenade. They did penetrate into the officers' flat passage through a window of the Chief Officer's suite but there was very little left to walk on. The wooden decking was burned through to the steel beneath, and that was red hot. Smoke, flame, scorching metal, ruin everywhere—and furthermore they had no lights. In the end they had to retreat without achieving their objective.

Garrett did try to enter the Empress Room below the bridge but he too was beaten back by flames flaring up to 3 or 4 feet high. Ransome and another man also reached the promenade deck before being forced back. But their efforts had not been in vain, because they found two passengers, unconscious but still alive, trapped on the forward promenade. If Ransome had not found them they would have died a very nasty death.

One of these was a Mrs Willis, wife of a Naval Stores Officer. The other was a sergeant who remains unnamed. Both were carried to the forward windows of the promenade, lowered into the hands of members of the party and eventually reached the temporary safety of the forecastle. Mrs Willis quickly recovered and was later well enough to clamber down a rope into a lifeboat—but not without further threats to her life, as will be seen. The sergeant had been badly hurt and was lashed to a door before being lowered. He was handed over to a military nurse working on the forecastle head.

* * *

Back on the after part of the boat deck, the starboard motorboat had been swung out. The area was now so thick with smoke that Commander Baker could hardly see the man on the winch. He himself entered the boat to assist a man trying to knock off the forward griping line. As far as Baker could see the only man giving instructions was a bosun's mate, and by the way he was carrying on Baker thought he had lost his nerve. This leading hand was shouting to the AB on the winch to let go, but Baker had different views. There were a lot of people who would want to use that boat and it would be useless to them if it was lowered to the water and allowed to drop astern. There were no ship's officers there, so Baker himself ordered the bosun's mate to get hold of himself and stop giving stupid orders. The boat would not be lowered until passengers were aboard it. But the AB did let go of the brake and down she went to the water. The winchman followed clambering down a rope.

Now the wind was rising—about Force 3, Baker thought— and the boat was not under control. But forward of them and also not yet under control, another lifeboat had broached to and was bearing down on them, beam on. Baker saw an accident coming, leapt to the helm and swung it over to give them a sheer, but he was too late. The lifeboat hit them beam on to their stem. The motor-boat was rising on a crest and miraculously it skidded right over. Baker could hardly believe his eyes.

Neither boat appeared badly damaged although the crew of the lifeboat—which was that of CPO Burley—had been tipped into the water, including Burley himself. When he came to the surface, the boat was some ten yards away but, surprisingly, still afloat. He swam to it and grabbed a lifeline. He was quickly hauled aboard and for some moments lay on the bottom exhausted. The First Officer was leaning over him trying to help but he himself was in great pain. Burley concluded that he had been hurt in the collision.

'You don't look too good yourself, Sir. Your arm . . .'

Keay admitted that he did not feel well and was in great pain. Burley arose and shakily helped him to a seat. 'You stay put, Sir. I'll look after this lot.'

As things turned out, Burley did indeed look after 'this lot' and did it very well, despite the sometimes reluctant attitude of the crew.

* * *

Chief Petty Officer Coward was on 'C' deck with the second class head steward, Mr Castles. 'Abandon Ship' had been signalled and there was nothing more they could do but get to their boats. Coward went up to 'A' deck via the Tourist stairway. Near the smoke room he came across the fire Bonwick had tried to put out. Wary of explosions in the magazine, he continued up past 'A' deck and then using the outside stairs climbed to the boat deck. There he joined CPO Jevans who, with two merchant seamen and a naval rating, was trying to lower the only pulling boat abaft the port side motor-boat.

Beneath this boat the sea was clear, but from a lower deck people were calling for help. They were hidden from the boat deck because of the overhang. Coward suggested that they should lower first to the after promenade and give anyone there a chance to come aboard, and then stop at any deck below where it was possible to help people. If it turned out to be unsafe to stop at any deck, then when they hit the water they should wait close in so that stranded passengers could climb down ropes.

Coward, Jevans, an RN rating and a merchant seaman jumped into the boat, leaving the other seaman to release the brake, and down she went—directly into the water, no attempt being made by the winchman to stop it at the promenade. He himself came down a rope. However, they were able to hold the boat close into the side and eventually seven ladies and one child came down. One of the ladies let go too soon and fell, hitting her head on a thwart. She was badly hurt. There was no first aid equipment on board and little they could do but bathe her head and make her as comfortable as possible. It seemed to Coward that a horde of seamen came down the ropes and boarded. There was also one army officer who entered the water and swam; this was Major Trotter.

By this time the boat was full, and as far as Coward could see no one was left on 'B' deck. There *were* people there, of course, but they were obscured by the height of the deck above them and by the overlaying smoke. In any case, the boat was full up and it was time to stand clear.

The two seamen whom Trotter had seen take charge were Coward and Jevans—both RN men.

Some yards from the ship they pulled two swimmers from the sea. There were plenty of able-bodied persons on board to handle oars, and Coward ordered his men to pull round to the starboard side of the *Empress* to enable him to make a lee.

* * *

The sun deck was burning fiercely, the tennis court an inferno with a huge hole in the middle. Petch and company had taken their injured mate, Andrews, to the boat deck and had laid him down alongside another injured man, AB Dunn, who had a broken leg.

Some action had been going on over at the starboard side motor-boat, but there was so much confusion and argument about who knew what best to do that Petch and his men gave up hope of ever getting into it. When it did eventually go down there were only three men aboard. Petch's comment was pure lower deck.

On the port side the other motor-boat had not been touched, perhaps because it had a hole in it. Still, it was a boat. They knew little about handling boats like this but at least they did it without confusion. The two wounded men were hoisted aboard; another lying nearby was also taken, but when he was found to be dead they put him back on deck.

A seaman of the ship's company arrived, went to the winch and helped them lower the boat. It slipped down smoothly at first, but suddenly gathered speed as the man at the winch let go.

'The winch bolts are starting—they're pulling out! Hold tight!'

There was a loud slap as the boat practically fell into the sea. Happily, it stayed afloat, the hole notwithstanding.

Once in the water others joined them, sliding down ropes. Among these was an engineer officer, the only ship's officer Petch had so far seen during the whole emergency. Fortunately this officer understood marine engines and it was he who, some ten minutes later, got the engine to start. Despite what Captain Sapsworth was to say later, it did appear that this boat had not been kept in good trim. Certainly it could not have been in the water for a considerable time, for under the impact of the descent three planks had sprung. This did not help very much, considering that there was already the hole in the stern.

They stuffed jerseys and oilskins into the hole and set about baling, using tin hats and a wooden box.

* * *

After its collision with Burley's boat, Commander Baker's motor-boat was still being towed by its fall. Then, to Baker's dismay, the deckhand under instruction from the bosun's mate released the fall and they began to drift. Baker reckoned at that time that the ship was still travelling at about 15 knots.

Differences in speeds estimated by various survivors throughout the action, like times, the number of bombs which fell, the type of bombs and so on, were notable. Fifteen knots when the engines had been stopped more than an hour before seems pretty high. Still, as noted earlier, the *Empress* had been making a top speed of 24 knots before abandoning. And most of these men were experts.

Of the three men in the boat, at that time only Baker knew anything about marine engines. This one he found obstinate, and its condition, like the one on the port side, was consistent with its not having been turned over or serviced for months. This was his own opinion. The Captain was to say in his sworn evidence that the motor-boats had been used at Suez, barely five weeks before, and that the engines, as reported to him, had been in good order then.

Unfortunately Baker had no tools and there was little he could do. But at some time during that frustrating morning, two other boats approached and in one of them there were both a Wireless Telegraphy officer, name unknown, and a Squadron Leader Harrison, RAF, who knew all about marine engines. Both were taken on board and put to work, although the Squadron Leader could do very little for his wrist was broken. He spent an agonizing half-hour tinkering as best he could with one hand but, like Baker, had no luck. The wireless officer did better. He erected an aerial and within a short period had the motor-boat's transmitting set working.

Up to this time they had no certain means of knowing whether the *Empress* had been able to send out distress signals, for the radio house could have been destroyed in the first attack when the bomb fell abaft of it. So they sent out their own signals. British planes had overflown the area before this, or at least one had—the Skua—so that the plight of the

Empress was known. Nevertheless, for 20 minutes they repeated: 'Empress of Britain bombed, on fire, west of Inishtrahull'.

Then the battery gave up.

* * *

The kerfuffle with Nos 2, 4 and 6 boats had been observed impatiently by Captain Sapsworth and he found reason for some critical comment to the Chief Officer who had rejoined him on the boat deck. Not that criticism helped them much because within minutes they were cut off from the boats by an eruption of fire and smoke which drove them back the way they had come. The Captain wondered what was going to happen to *him*. It all seemed very unfair. His wonder increased when through the quite impassable fire stretching from rail to bulkhead he saw the arrival of the Commodore with three men at the rail on the other side of the fire, and 30 feet abaft of him. He shouted to them but they did not hear.

The Commodore had given up his fire-fighting, had collected the bosun and two signalmen of his own staff, and had made for safety. From the rail he saw the ladder hanging over No 4 boat. He noted the argument between Hitchener and Morison about the positions of Nos 4 and 6, seized the opportunity and climbed down the ladder followed by his companions. Shortly after, whilst Hitchener was explaining why he could not slip, Nicholson took command. He ordered Hitchener to let go and away went No 4. They fell astern quickly, handed along from rope to rope until they were clear. Hitchener went forward and from the prow helped drag swimmers from the sea.

The Captain, in spite of the overhang of the promenade deck, could see well enough what was going on and it was with mixed feelings that he watched the Commodore take command of No 4 and sail away whilst he, the Captain, was left in a most precarious position high up on a blazing boat deck. Again, it all seemed very unfair.

On the winch, Fourth Officer Howell released the brake of No 6. Abaft of his position, an AB was struggling with the winch of No 8. Sapsworth and Davies could reach neither. They watched No 6 take to the water directly below the ladder Nicholson and his party had climbed down.

Howell and Morison must now have been about 30 feet

away from the Captain and cut off from him by the fire which had also separated him from Nicholson. Whilst Morison was busy—quite apart from his concern for his Captain—with helping the AB lower No 8, Howell wanted to get down into No 6 which was being handled with great difficulty by those who had boarded her. But he was also aware of the Captain's hazardous situation, and he shouted to him that if he could climb outside the rail and along the fishplate he might get past the fire and reach the ladder. Even whilst they were shouting these instructions to one another, No 8 went down to the sea. The Chief Officer looked to the Captain for a lead.

'There's nothing more we can do here, Sir.'

The Captain nodded. The Chief led the way, climbing the rail and edging precariously past the flames. Sapsworth waited for him to get onto the ladder to climb down to No 6. Unfortunately the ladder was partially burned through and the Chief decided not to risk it. Stanley now joined his Captain in edging along the outside of the rail. Once in a favourable position he hopped back over, grabbed a rope, hitched it to the rail, dropped one end to the boat and urged Sapsworth to climb down. Sapsworth allowed Davies to go first and then followed. But such was their luck on this most luckless of all days for them, that a boat rope of No 6 which had been holding her to the ship through a promenade window, now burned through and she pulled away, dragging on her falls. Someone in the boat decided it was time to go. They slipped and away went No 6 leaving the Captain, the Chief Officer and Mr Stanley hanging in mid-air, halfway, as it were, between the heavens and the waters under the heavens. The Captain was not amused.

But still there was No 8. This was still being handled by the struggling AB. He had lowered it somewhat hurriedly under Morison's instructions and it was now in the water being towed by its rope. Howell and Morison decided the best thing to do was at least to try to haul it forward under the Captain's rope. In the circumstances, in a rising sea and with the ship's way still at about 5 knots, the only way to do this was to get it as close to the ship's side as possible and shorten the rope with all hands pulling. They hoped the Captain would understand that he might have to enter the water and swim if the way proved too strong.

But in the midst of these goings-on a new problem arose.

Someone was now heard to be shouting frantically through the porthole of a cabin on 'A' deck some 35 feet above sea level. The construction of the ship was such that it was not possible to see what was going on from above because the intervening promenade deck overhung 'A' deck by some feet. Morison flung another rope over and climbed down to see what the fuss was all about.

A group of people were trapped in the cabin unable to get past the fires in the alleyway, and the future for them looked bleak. The only hope they had was to squeeze out through the porthole. This, as anyone who has tried it under stress will know, is not an easy thing to do.

Morison told them to hang on, and to keep the cabin door shut tight so that there would be no draught to encourage the fires in the alleyway. He began his upward climb with the intention of finding ropes to lower to these unfortunate persons. He did not make it. His rope, already partly burned, began to fray and he did the only sensible thing. He slid down helter skelter, fortunately coming to rest with his feet on a thwart of No 8. From here he shouted to Howell, explaining the situation in the 'A' deck cabin. Howell himself could not see because of the overhang, but under guidance from Morison he flung down ropes to hang as close to the porthole as possible and fastened his ends to a davit.

Those in the cabin now had to face the chancy business of hooking the ropes, pulling them in, climbing out of the porthole and going hand over hand down to No 8 boat. One shudders to think what would have happened to them had Morison not heard their shouts.

One of these persons was Lord Yarborough. And as he climbed through the porthole with his feet trailing behind him, something fell from above and hit him on the head, and for the rest of his life he was fond of telling the story of how this unspecified, but somehow hilarious, object had come out of the blue and 'crowned him Lord of all'.

The situation now was that on the port side Nos 2, 4, 6 and 8 were in the water. Nos 2, 4 and 6 had drifted away. The Captain, the Chief Officer and Second Officer were clinging hopefully to their rope. Morison was in No 8 and seriously concerned about the unfortunate position the Captain found himself in and felt it would be unfair to tell him he would have to drop to the water and swim. But the Chief Officer, Mr Davies at the bottom of the rope did just that and he was safely hauled aboard.

Mr Howell now came clambering down a rope followed by the AB. They had left the boat deck abaft of the Captain's rope, with the flames virtually licking their heels.

Together, those now in No 8 successfully pulled the boat forward beneath the Captain and he descended with Stanley following him. Like Joan Stephenson, despite all the hazard and inconvenience, neither even got their feet wet.

It was a strange climax and for the Captain, unlike the Earl, in no way amusing. He assumed command of the boat.

Howell reckoned that the ship's speed at the time was about 4 knots. As they drifted away from the side, Sapsworth for the first time saw something of the large crowd of people hanging over the rails of the forewelldeck and forecastle. Their circumstances were so obviously hazardous that he urged his officers to try to pull forward and get under the bows. And despite the rising wind, the increasingly choppy sea and the ship's way, they must have succeeded in halting their drift to some extent, for several people did come down ropes and ladders, enter the water and swim towards them. Among the latter were a Mr Willis, the Naval Stores Officer from Cape Town, and his daughter. They must have had an anxious swim for they had, according to a report later put in by Mr Willis, entered the water from the forecastle and swum to the boat drifting amidships, some several hundred yards, through a rising sea and against the boat's drift.

The Captain's boat continued to drift. As they passed the stern someone on the capstan deck ('B' deck) hailed them, but it was too late and they drifted away.

* * *

Keay's boat, or perhaps more correctly now, CPO Burley's boat—for Keay was incapacitated and Burley to all intents and purposes was in command—was some three-quarters of a mile astern of the *Empress*. He had 15 men on board, at least two of them injured—Keay and an unnamed serjeant. Burley realized that they could not just hang about when all boats were so obviously needed urgently back at the ship. At a pinch he could take another 80 men, men who without help might very easily die. He stated the position to the men. Unfortunately, some merchant seamen among the crew did not want to go back because they feared that the *Empress* was about to blow up. And, indeed, even at this distance the repeated explosions were loud and threatening. They wanted no part in it.

And in this respect, and from the author's observation, and without understating the overall high standards of the merchant service during the Second World War, it was true that some merchant seamen did not live up to the reputation bestowed upon the service as a whole, and cases of 'I'm alright, Jack,' and greed and exploitation of troops on troopships occurred not infrequently.

Burley was supported by Keay and the serjeant, and the dissidents were shamed into compliance. Six oars were manned—damage done to the boat during the collision with the motor-boat prevented more being used. They pulled towards the *Empress*.

Midday: In the water

There is no absolute way of establishing exact times of events during this tragedy. No one seemed to know what the time was or even to remember clearly what the sequence of events was or how long they lasted. Certain things happened and they all happened within a few hours. So that, for example, when we say that it was at about 1100 that Rona Trotter, hanging onto her rope and hovering a few feet above the surging sea, discovering that her rope was burning through, it might have been either earlier or later. It does not really matter, but it helps keep the whole story in perspective.

Suddenly she and her seaman companion had no option but to enter the water. She handed her flask of brandy to the seaman, said goodbye to her handbag containing the revolver and the £100, and together these two souls struck out towards a raft flopping about empty some 200 yards away. Fortunately Rona Trotter was a strong swimmer and had little fear of water, and in the end they made the journey despite the difficulties of cold, wind, waves and current. She remained for some time in the water hanging onto a lifeline but she does not now, or perhaps did not even then, remember for how long.

It appears that her companion must have been able, with her assistance, to clamber aboard, at which stage he would then have been able, in his turn to help her. Anyone who has ever tried to climb from the sea onto a raft without help, particularly in difficult weather and in a freezing sea, will know how extremely difficult, if not impossible, it is. They remained on the raft for several hours.

* * *

A very worried Ransome was leaning over the port side rail of the forecastle looking back towards the centre of the ship. A jumping ladder hung down from the forward part of the promenade deck. It was cut off by smoke and flame fore and aft and was loaded from top to bottom with men trying to escape the fire trap. It is possible that these were some of the men Captain Sapsworth had seen in a huddle on his way to the boats and who had, after all, found no means of escape.

On the ladder there was a lot of argument, foul language induced by panic, and some shoving, kicking and treading on hands. It was a most tragic scene. It sickened Ransome and he would have liked to help them. But even as he watched, some of these unfortunate men, either because they were pushed, trodden on or maybe had just given up, hurtled down into the water. Someone—perhaps Ransome and an assistant—threw over one of the home-made rafts, hoping it would drift back to these men. It came apart as it hit the water and the struggling men had to grab such bits and pieces as they could.

About a mile to a mile and a half away some lifeboats were lying apparently stationary in the water. As far as Ransome could see there were only a few persons in them, too few to handle oars to bring them back. He had the idea that if they called for volunteers among the strong swimmers they might be able to reach one of the boats, add their strength to that of those on board and bring at least one of them back.

Garrett had no illusions about what was happening. He knew quite well that within an hour or so, if they had that much time, the flames would engulf them. Their's would be the choice of remaining on board to be incinerated or going over the side to whatever fate might await them there. Inevitably many lives would be lost.

Ransome's suggestion was a desperate one. To jump 40 feet

into an icy and choppy sea and then swim a mile or so to a boat the swimmer would not be able to see except perhaps from crests of waves, was hazardous to say the least of it.

'We might get one of them back, Sir.'

'We might. A mighty big might. You volunteering, Chief?'

It was a possibility and Ransome was a reliable and resourceful man. If anyone could do it, Ransome could.

He was joined by three other volunteers, one of them an AB named Giles, the others unknown. They went down to the sea on a rope with Ransome leading. Garrett had a raft dropped over to them. If they could swim with it before them at least it would give them some security. But, of course, the raft was hopeless. It was impossible to guide it, it prevented them seeing where they were going, and in any case it would have taken an eternity. They swam on alone.

It was not too long before they lost their bearings, as was to be expected, since they had only the *Empress* behind them to guide them. Ransome soon found he was on his own. He gave up and just floated on the rising and falling waves. He had no idea at that time of what had happened to Giles and the other men.

* * *

The importance of the role their motor-boat could play was not lost upon Petch and his companions. They realized that such a vessel—*if it were in good shape*—could prove vital in towing drifting lifeboats back to the ship. But their boat was not in good shape. Water was coming through the hole, (despite the plug of oilskins) and through the sprung boards, and they had to bale continuously. It looked as if it would be a losing battle. In any case, within a few minutes of the first successful response from the engine, it coughed and stopped. Steam rose from the engine housing as water entered.

Their major worry was what would happen to their injured men if they themselves had to take to the water and swim. They kept on baling even though they barely managed to maintain any freeboard.

At last a boat approached near enough to them to be hailed. This was the Captain's boat with a number of his executive officers on board, a point which raised some comment amongst disgruntled survivors later. Petch asked the Captain if they could move over to his boat, but this was deemed impossible since it appeared that the Captain's boat was already over-loaded. But the state of the motor-boat being what it was, he agreed to take the wounded and they were duly passed over. From that point Petch and his mates just had to sweat it out. It was a long, arduous and chancy sweat.

There was still some 20 men on board, and faced with the certainty that their boat must sink, they tried to keep close to other boats. It was not easy, for their own boat was water-logged, they were taking on water moment by moment, there was little freeboard and the stern was very low in the water. They had no oars and paddling with their hands gave them barely any movement. Overall, they had little control. There was little they could do other than keep on baling.

The water crept in slowly but remorselessly, gradually tip-ping up the prow as the stern sank deeper. Any move they made had to be with the greatest caution. And in the end the sea won.

The hole suddenly gulped water, air bubbled up, there was a sickening rise in the prow and a movement as though she would roll over on one side. Then down went the stern and over she rolled. In doing so she must have trapped some air under the stern, for she remained mainly submerged but still floating. Petch and company were thrown into the sea.

They came to the surface spitting water, numb with cold but relieved still to find the boat near them and afloat, although keel uppermost. How long it would remain so was anybody's guess. Any shift in the water could easily drain air. How long? No one cared to think about it.

They held on to whatever parts they could. The lifelines were useless because now most of them were below the surface and gave no support. In any case, any weight on them could only upset the delicate balance, turn the boat onto one side and send it under. It was an extremely difficult situation—not for them all, of course, for many of them had gone. The time? Possibly 1245.

* * *

Back to George Bonwick. It was some time before another lifeboat approached close enough to the after parts of the ship to be hailed. But there was no joy for Bonwick. It seemed to him that those on the lifeboat were not organized and their boat was being allowed to slip astern of the *Empress* with nothing being done to prevent it. It is quite probable that this was the Captain's boat. The timing would be about right, and at the Board of Enquiry Captain Sapsworth did say that his boat had drifted under the stern.

Bonwick then had to wait another hour, expecting every moment to be blown skyhigh, for the explosions on 'A' deck persisted. But at—possibly—1230 someone must have broken through the fire at the after end of the port side of the boat deck, because suddenly a boat was lowered. This was, presumably, No 18, positioned just abaft of the after funnel. It could hardly have been any other because, whilst we know that Nos 2, 4, 6 and 8 had been lowered, they being the only ones on the port side forward which had not been destroyed either by burning or by bomb blast; and since on the after port side, the motor-boat and the pulling boat abaft of it had got away, the only other boat which might have avoided destruction was the one forward of the motor-boat, that is No 18.

Bonwick hailed the cox'n, ordering him to pull alongside. He then slung mooring lines over the side and made them fast. There was a discarded canvas hose which he also used.

Meanwhile the boat was now flopping about close in, and in some difficulty because of the whipped-up sea. A man in the boat was fending off as best he could to prevent the boat crashing into the ship's side. It had a considerable number of people on board and by the time Bonwick had persuaded his ladies to climb down his ropes into the boat it was at capacity. He ordered the cox'n away but instructed him to send back any boats he saw which were only partly filled.

* * *

There was a stiff wind blowing, forming white crests as Captain Sapsworth's boat drifted past the stern. They could see a number of people on 'B' deck. One of these must have been George Bonwick, and the Captain's boat the one which did not respond to his shouts for assistance.

In private conversation with the author, George Bonwick was often a little strained in his comments concerning Captain Sapsworth for a number of reasons, and perhaps one of them was that he had not responded to Bonwick's call for help. But

Sapsworth said he did go back under the stern. He also said that there was another boat there at the time, and that he had gained the impression that it took off the last of those stranded there. But, incomprehensibly, Captain Sapsworth also said in his evidence that shortly after he left the *Empress* the ammunition blew up and *'must have blown half the stern out of her'*.

One wonders where he got that one from. In fact, the stern did not blow up at all, and for some considerable time after Sapsworth had gone there were many people on the deck below the magazine who were eventually taken off in lifeboats.

In any event, it seems that the Captain must have ordered his boat away and later was able to see clearly the position of all still stranded on the *Empress*, fore and aft. It was at about this time that he took Petch's wounded on board. The time was perhaps about 12 noon.

* * *

For some time Delorme had been in the process of evacuating his patients from the hospital. No one had heard 'Abandon Ship' signalled, but there was no doubt in anyone's mind about what was going on. The doctor had mustered his staff and voluntary helpers and between them they took all stretcher cases up via the Tourist stairway to the starboard side of 'B' shelter deck. Here, compared to other parts of the ship, it was relatively clear of smoke.

Fires were burning forward of them along the engineers' alleyway, whilst the doctor's own quarters on the port side had disappeared under smoke and seemed likely to burst into flame at any moment. But outside, abaft the after lounge, apart from periodic clouds of smoke and airborne fragments of burning material caught by the draught, things were not too bad—that is, if one could ignore the ammunition exploding in the lockers above them.

Incidentally, Delorme was comforted by one 'old naval sweat' who assured him that the explosions were only fuses burning and that the shells themselves would not go off, so it was alright. Fine! But Delorme could not help looking at a 'No Smoking' sign slowly peeling off the bulkhead under the heat and wondering whether it might not be better to be blown up and get the thing over with, rather than being drowned or barbecued slowly.

In any case, earlier, with the flames in 'B' deck passages sweeping back towards them, the threat had been sufficient to convince some daring souls that drowning might be preferable. They went over the side and swam. Some of them did drown.

Among those who went over the side were Evans, the Second Engineer, and Redmund, his Chief. Evans was fortunate and made a hazardous but successful swim to a lifeboat. Redmund disappeared. Before they had made the decision to go, Delorme had discussed the idea with Redmund and had warned him not to take the chance. Redmund was not young, it was a cold winter sea, and the nearest boat at that time probably half a mile away and drifting.

It seems that Bonwick must still have been on 'B' deck at that time and had seen Redmund but was not involved in the discussion. He was, however, suddenly aware that Evans and Redmund were no longer with them, and he formed the impression that they had gone below in a final attempt to do something about the pumps. Mission impossible, of course, but Bonwick was not an engineer. It was 44 years later that George Bonwick learned what had happened to the Chief Engineer, and only then when the author told him. Bonwick said, 'Redmund was a fine man. What a waste!'

Mr Evans wore a standard Board of Trade-type lifejacket and this, apart from his comparative youth, was probably the major factor enabling him to reach a boat safely. Whether or not Redmund wore a lifejacket is not known. His body was never found. It seems probable that if he had worn a lifejacket and had collapsed from exhaustion, his body would have floated and someone might have found him even though he were dead. Because they did not, it is likely that he ignored an elementary factor of safety at sea and went into the water unsupported. But no one knows.

The boat Evans reached was a small one designed to hold about 45 men. Quartermaster Reynolds was the cox'n in charge. They pulled slowly back towards the ship, picking up four swimmers on the way. Their complement was then 30 persons.

They reached the stern of the *Empress* at about 1300. Bonwick and Delorme were still standing at the rail, terribly conscious of the flames now so close to them. They shouted at Reynolds to come alongside, saying that they had a number of stretcher cases. The boat pulled in. Again Bonwick cut lines from fog-buoys and flung them over, and with their help the stretchers were lowered.

Bonwick then noticed that the men in the boat were becoming edgy. Above them the wing of the docking bridge, badly damaged by the bomb which destroyed the 3-inch gun, was hanging precariously over the edge of the after promenade deck. If part of the structure fell, it could easily smash their boat, and certainly would kill or injure many of those on board. Anyone of the explosions in the magazine might send it hurtling down, for already burning fragments were falling.

Bonwick acted quickly. That boat was going to take his people, come what may. He grabbed one of the lines and swung himself downwards, determined to take over command from whoever was in charge. It was doubtful who that might have been. Certainly Quartermaster Reynolds was at the tiller, but there was an engineer officer there too, and although he did not appear to be taking much part he was certainly senior to Reynolds and should have been able to ensure that everyone did their duty. Bonwick acted with authority and quickly established that he was in command—which was not bad for an insignificant Fifth Officer. Four more stretchers were lowered. There was still room for seven more passengers.

But for Bonwick, being down in the boat was a different thing to being Bonwick up on 'B' deck. The wing of the docking bridge was swinging loose, parts of it flopping about in the wind. Stanchions had been twisted away, bolts had sprung, part of the rail had become detached. It was something of a dilemma. If he ordered the boat away—which seemed the best thing to do—it might be said that he had deserted his charges to save his own skin. He shouted up at the assembled faces that he would have to move a short distance away and they would have to come down the ropes, enter the water and swim to him. He would make sure they were hauled aboard.

His boat then pulled a little astern. But at this moment another lifeboat came around the stern from starboard. Bonwick directed Reynolds to approach the new arrival so that they could tell them about the people still on 'B' deck. In the meantime, Bonwick's men pulled two swimmers from the sea—Dr Greig of the RAMC and one other, name not known.

The newly arrived boat then pulled in a little way abaft the docking bridge and some yards out.

* * *

The Captain's boat was pretty well loaded, its complement now including the Chief Officer, the Second, Third, Fourth and Sixth Officers and of course, the Captain. It was quite a distinguished load and became the subject of some odd comment later on when the question was raised about the number of executive officers in one boat when other survivors had not set eyes on a single ship's officer during the entire action. But these comments were unfair, as examination of the officers' actions described earlier reveals. The complement also included several swimmers taken from the sea, not forgetting the two wounded men taken from Petch and company's motor-boat.

During the morning a number of corpses floated by, most of them unrecognizable, although Mansell did place one of them. This was a Mr Till who had been a waiter in the first class saloon and one of Mansell's fire-fighting party.

But among the floating corpses were two which suddenly came to life. After having been regarded as just another couple of bodies, they suddenly began shouting and waving. The Captain's boat pulled towards them and they were hauled aboard. They were CPO Ransome and one of his party, AB Giles. They were cold, wet, miserable and weary. They had managed to keep themselves afloat by lying supine and keeping their hands and feet moving. Somehow, after being forced to abandon their desperate mission in retrieving a lifeboat and being separated, they had found one another again. They were the lucky ones, or so it is assumed, for nothing is known of what happened to the other men who set off with them. Perhaps they just drifted away and were lost. Perhaps they were picked up and eventually were taken ashore, just a couple of anonymous heroes, quiet men with a sense of duty who did what they did without thought of recognition, or even consciousness that they were doing something worthy of special recognition.

The *Empress* now lay about a mile on the Captain's port quarter. She was still belching huge clouds of smoke. There were fires blazing on the forward decks, the promenade and boat deck. She was still burning amidships.

Several hundred frightened refugees were crowded on the forecastle and forecastle head, wondering why they alone had been forsaken. They could see and know nothing of what was going on in other parts of the ship.

* * *

Petch and Company were still grimly hanging on to whichever parts of the capsized motor-boat they could grab. They did not know if anyone was aware of their desperate plight, and certainly no one came to their rescue.

At about 1330 both a Wellington bomber and a Sunderland flying boat flew over, circled the ship and signalled that help was on the way. The Commander of the Sunderland was especially kind to Petch and Company, for in a most timely gesture he dropped off a rubber lifeboat. It was the only good thing that had happened to these men since breakfast. But it went wrong. The pilot misjudged the wind and the boat dropped to leeward and simply floated away. It was all a bit much.

But Pullen did not give up. He let go his grip on the boat and swam for the dinghy. He swam strongly but it was just not good enough, for the boat, presenting a light and broad surface to the wind, plopped persistently away. After several minutes poor Pullen had to give up and swim back towards the motor-boat. But by now he was worn out and after a while he decided to rest. Disastrously, he just lay there floating. But the sea and its currents were cruel, and when he awoke to the realization of what was happening, he was 100 yards or more away from his mates. He made a desperate struggle back, the threat of blind panic increasing with every stroke. At last, utterly exhausted, he threw his arms upwards and submitted to death. But Hipwell, seeing what was happening to this man, left his own dangerous security, swam to him and hauled him back to the motor-boat. Grimly he clung to the boat with one hand and to Pullen with the other.

For almost four hours they held on like that, and despite boats coming within reasonable proximity, none came to their rescue.

* * *

When Commodore Nicholson took charge of No 4, Petty Officer Hitchener moved to the bows where he helped pull swimmers from the sea. They identified explosions on the after deck as ammunition going off spontaneously, and decided that the stern of the *Empress* was a good place to keep away from, although there were people hanging over 'B' deck rail obviously in trouble. The fact was that No 4 was not yet organized.

By the time they were able to make a real effort to return, they were a long way astern, possibly more than a mile. Of the 25 men aboard, for one reason or another only eight were capable of pulling oars. Progress was slow.

At one time they passed fairly close to Baker's motor-boat, and the Commodore thought to approach it and order it to take him, and any other boats they might pass, in tow. But he was pre-empted by Baker's semaphore signal asking for an engineer and tools. Nicholson was unable to help. He took his boat on her way.

One of the men Hitchener had pulled from the water was Colonel Peake of the RAMC, a doctor. He was exhausted and at that time incapable of helping fellow passengers. Later this doctor did some very good work.

Nicholson reckoned it was at about 1300 that the Wellington bomber came over, although others thought it was more probably 1330. But no one really knew what the time was. As with the Skua, it is difficult to see what help a Wellington bomber could be, but it was reassuring at least to know that their plight was not being ignored. Also, of course, the plane may have been looking for enemy U-boats sniffing around the area. As will be seen, there was good reason for this.

They cleared the stern of the *Empress* and approached the port bow. The rail was full of people shouting and waving.

* * *

Neither Rona Trotter nor her seaman companion remembered how long they were on their raft. It must have been at least two hours and certainly it was long enough for them to resort to a swig or so from the brandy flask.

In the end a lifeboat did come close enough for them to risk a further dangerous swim. It seems likely that this boat was George Bonwick's, although today he does not remember the lady. Debatably, Bonwick's boat came around the stern at about 1345 and he says that subsequently he picked up people from rafts. He quotes four men. But he said he also picked up swimmers, and Mrs Trotter and her companion did swim from their raft to a lifeboat.

Speaking in 1983, Mrs Askew (Mrs Trotter as she was) knew that the boat she swam to was neither the Captain's nor the First Officer's nor the Commodore's. It could not have been the doctor's because when later he transferred from one boat to another to help a dying man, Mrs Trotter was on the boat he transferred to. Clearly she was not on either of the two motor-boats. Others that might have been available were the pulling boat from abaft the port side motor-boat and No 18.

The former was in charge of CPO Jevans and CPO Coward. It is unlikely that Mrs Trotter was with them because Major Trotter *was*, and in spite of the confusion it is quite certain that they were not in the same lifeboat. In fact, Trotter had no idea where his sister-in-law was until he met her later on board a rescuing destroyer. The probability is that she was with Bonwick.

When Garrett at one time during this extraordinary day counted the boats which he could see floating about at various distances from the *Empress*, he arrived at a figure of about nine. All are accounted for except No 2—one of the smaller boats forward on the boat deck, port and starboard—*unless* No 2 was Bonwick's boat which *is* accounted for. We know that Bonwick was on one of the smaller boats because the boat to which he had swung down had Evans the Second Engineer on board and was said to have been capable of carrying only 45 passengers.

The other small boat, that on the starboard side (No 1), must have been the boat Ransome and Garrett had unsuccessfully tried to reach, because it was right forward on the starboard side.

There are other factors. After being hauled aboard with the seaman, the lady had asked him for the flask of brandy. He had lost it, which was rather bad luck, for at this stage another good hearty swig would have been just the thing. The thought that the seaman himself had emptied it during his swim is an unworthy one. Still, Rona was annoyed. But anyway, the idea was a good one and Bonwick (it must have been he) hailed a nearby boat asking if they had any spirits for his exhausted passengers. The nearby boat was Delorme's.

All of which is probably unimportant except that it does lead up to a story told by Dr Delorme. He tells of '. . . another outstanding action which I witnessed only in part but which was reported to me by a number of witnesses . . . a Mrs Rona Trotter returning from the Middle East . . . was in a party taken off the forepart of the ship and as a strong swimmer took it upon herself to swim between boats picking up exhausted swimmers and towing them to safety. She was seen to carry out several of these rescues, and when I saw her she was lying exhausted in the bow of a lifeboat. The man she was trying to keep warm I found to be dead.'

Dr Delorme seems to have got some of this story wrong or else the lady did not clearly remember, because Mrs Askew denied that she did any such thing except that she did admit to having helped one person swim to a lifeboat. And, of course, she was not taken off the forepart of the ship. She went down a rope, swam to a raft and after a number of hazards made it to a lifeboat which seems to have been George Bonwick's and was taken aboard, unfortunately without her brandy.

Until they were rescued she said they sang 'Roll out the Barrel' and kindred songs of those exciting times, including 'We'll hang out our washing on the Siegfried Line'.

How long ago it all seems, with this brave lady now dead after partial paralysis from a stroke; and Bonwick living comfortably (and somewhat aggressively, judging by what happens at the shipping company Annual General Meetings he attends) in his pleasant home in Wokingham where, oddly enough, according to his wife Betty, his major occupation outside of shipping is the contemplation of his future death, an event he looks forward to with disquiet. One can only hope that his disquiet does not arise from a misguidedly guilty conscience. Then Dr Delorme is ensconced in his markedly batchelor basement flat in London SW7, after a lifetime of successful surgery, research and teaching medicine; Jimmy England perhaps looking down at them all over a tubby paunch from some salt-water Valhalla.

* * *

Commander Garrett and Purser Pearch had done all they could. Pearch was despondent and, indeed, not far from panic, for the fires were encroaching upon their hazardous refuge on the forecastle. Huge flames were flaring up from No 2 Hold and the forward lounge. There seemed to be no way out. Thick yellow-tinged smoke overhung the entire foreparts of the ship, turning daylight into darkness. There was no way of fighting the approaching fires and no way to dodge them except to crowd nearer to the forecastle head and the threat of the 40-foot jump beyond it. There was no other way.

Garrett had the additional anxiety about Ransome, Giles and the other brave men who had swum out to the unknown, and was cursing the culpabilities of the people in charge who had left the ship so open to this tragedy. It was unfair, of course, for who could have foreseen the effect of that first bomb? But then again, *was* it really unfair? One might not have foreseen the effect of a bomb, but at least, in this war at sea, surely this great ship should have been separated from its peacetime fun and games and prepared for such a tragedy as was destroying her now.

But the good Lord looks after the sea-going faithful especially the helpless ones who ask for help, and at this time, approximately 1345, a lifeboat came out of the blanket of smoke on the port side closely hugging the hull to creep round to the starboard bow where, on the windward side, the air was clear. It was No 4.

It appeared to both Pearch and Garrett that there were two men in charge—the bosun astern at the tiller and a naval Petty Officer in the bows who was fending off with an oar. This was Hitchener. Neither Garrett nor Pearch discovered that the Commodore was on board until it left the ship's side loaded with refugees—which again is unfair, because their attention was being paid to the embarkation. In any case, with the bosun in the stern and Hitchener in the bows, both doing the important jobs, what really was there for the Commodore to do except to help seat the passengers?

The first to come down were the wounded. In time-honoured fashion the women and children followed. Garrett was supervizing the disembarkation from the forecastle as one would have expected, and with the boat filled to capacity he instructed the bosun to pull away but to stay in the area in case those left on board had to take to the water. Swimmers might not be able to get aboard but they could hang on to lifelines.

Hitchener shoved his oar into the ship's side and pushed her away, flinging the ladder back to the hull. Once away from the ship, the Commodore remembered the motor-boat which had asked for help. He decided that having got his boat loaded with survivors, the best thing he could do was to backtrack, find the motor-boat and get its motor working. To his mind it was more important that the motor-boat should be made available for towing pulling boats, than that his boat should hang about doing nothing until it might be required. One wonders who was right—Garrett or Nicholson. Probably, as it turned out, Nicholson was, but one may imagine the anger of the frustrated Garrett as he saw No 4 pull away astern.

* * *

In the meantime CPO Coward's boat had also fallen well astern. There were now two other CPOs with him, and after consultation they decided to get round to windward of the *Empress* so that they could drift in towards her. There were a number of other boats both ahead and astern, probably Nos 2, 4 and 6.

Coward's men pulled steadily back towards the windward side of the ship and at about 1300 (according to Jevans) they saw a lifeboat alongside the ship on the starboard side taking refugees from the after decks. Ammunition was still exploding and Coward decided to stay clear.

They pulled into the wind and edged in cautiously. Now they saw a boat close in under the starboard bow of the *Empress* and people climbing down ropes into it. Their own boat being well loaded, Coward considered it best to wait in the vicinity and not go in too close unless it became obvious that they were needed.

* * *

At about 1345 the remnants of Delorme's party and others were still on 'B' deck. All stretcher cases had gone away on Bonwick's boat but there was still a considerable number of persons left wondering what was going to happen, their fears heightened by the nerve-racking explosions overhead and the flames creeping up on them from the 'B' deck alleyways and the after lounge.

Then, as Delorme puts it, they had an incredible stroke of

luck. Forward, along the after part of the starboard side, most of the boats had been consumed in the fires. Some had been left hanging from their davits when attempts to lower them had been abandoned. But one, slightly abaft the rear funnel, had been lowered to the promenade deck where it remained out of reach. It had not burned and hung there by its falls.

At last the flames crept up to it, got at the fall cables and burned them away, the boat fell plumb into the sea. Miraculously it did not take water. A party of seamen trapped between the engineers' smoking room and the position of this boat seized the chance to save their lives, fought their way to a landing port on 'B' deck, flung ropes over, hurled themselves downwards and swam to the lifeboat. There is no doubt that this fortuitous incident saved them from being either incinerated or having to leap into the dangerous sanctuary of an inhospitable sea. The same choice seemed to lie ahead for Delorme and his companions.

The men now in the boat fended it away and began dropping astern. Fortunately, Delorme was able to bring their attention to those still stranded and they pulled in as close as they dare, wary of the ammunition still exploding. Dr Delorme describes what happened:

'. . . our only sensible course had been to sweat it out and hope for some of the boats to return for us. But at about 1230 [It would have been nearer 1345] we had an incredible stroke of luck. Most of the boats which had not been launched had been damaged or burnt, but now one that had been only partially lowered and was hanging from its davits was released by the fire reaching its falls so that the boat fell into the sea. Some crew had been trapped forward of us and went through a landing port and reached her. This boat came to take us off but stood clear because of the exploding shells (not to mention the docking bridge!) so we had to swim for it. A number of those who were a bit too keen slid down the ropes 40 feet or so and burned their hands badly but no one complained of that.

'At the last minute we were almost sunk when a heavy shell casing fell into the sea close to our boat which raised a great cheer, an example of that curious hilarity which accompanies sudden release from danger.'

It seemed almost as though King Neptune had frowned on their last-moment escape and had taken a parting shot. And it is true that what Dr Delorme called 'a curious hilarity' does accompany an escape from great fear, whether of death or whatever. Usually it is followed by a deep inner silence and often by depression. It was so with released prisoners of war in the Far East, witnessed by the author. After the first bursts of glee and euphoria (the 'curious hilarity'), the sudden easing of the struggle to keep hope strong in the face of a fearful and uncertain future, often with the nightmare dread of insanity, was followed by an intense lowering of purpose and spirit.

The doctor was one of the last of his special party to leave the ship. Mr Moss, the Chief Steward, was with him. Because they were concerned that there might be injured people in other boats needing the doctor's attention, the man acting as cox'n was instructed to steer towards boats congregated about half a mile away from the *Empress*. The time was probably about 1400.

* * *

One of the men who slid down into the sea and swam to Delorme's boat was Seaman Webb. He had been a member of the gun crew with Petch and company. Webb, Delorme and Moss, the Chief Steward, were the last to leave the after part of the ship, following a French officer, General Gentilhomme who had come all the way from French Somaliland to get mixed up in a situation like this and who was later to become famous as a Free French officer under De Gaulle.

There were, Webb thought, between 80 and 90 persons on board, mainly ship's personnel but with some Royal Navy and military men. Webb did not think the boat was unreasonably overcrowded, for all this. Later he was to say he was a little ashamed of the undisciplined behaviour on board with at first no one appearing to know what to do. The doctor still had his dispenser and assistant with him and had been concerned to get to other boats which might need him but even he, Webb thought, did nothing to establish discipline. In the end, Webb said, an elderly seaman took charge and got the men to the oars.

This elderly seaman was Mr Moss (Webb thought his name was Marsh), and it was he who put a man in the prow to keep a look-out for wreckage and swimming survivors, and in this way, despite the number already on board, they picked up a number of persons.

Dr Delorme himself took over an oar. He was later to say that he did this because he was cold, but it is possible that not being the sort of person who could easily take over leadership in this sort of situation—for he is a shy and undemonstrative man—he preferred to pull his weight in other ways.

Webb says that the doctor and his assistants had very little equipment or medical materials with them, but despite this the doctor insisted that they steer to other boats to see if his help was needed.

There were still people on the forecastle head and the doctor suggested to Moss that they go over to see if they could help, but this was not done. They were already over their complement and in any case there was, as the cox'n pointed out, another boat coming round the bows of the *Empress* and pulling close.

Shortly, after a great deal of shouting, people were climbing down rope ladders into what was probably CPO Burley's boat.

* * *

The Purser and his deputy, grimly standing guard over their canvas bags, were still on the forecastle with Garrett. The latter was obsessed with his worry about Ransome and angry because No 4 boat had chosen to ignore his request and gone off into the blue. And then suddenly the situation changed, for Burley's boat was approached on the leeward side (the *Empress* having shifted), the wind still coming from the south-east.

Keay and Burley had had a pretty challenging time. Keay with his broken arm had squatted sick and exhausted at the rear of the boat, virtually incapacitated, although doing what he could to help Burley. The men had been restive and had only been persuaded to return to the vicinity of the ship by Burley's forcibly worded and extremely Royal Navy-fashioned insults and his decisive refusal to argue with them.

They pulled for the ship, carefully avoiding the potential volcano at the stern. When he was 50 yards off the ship's port side and abreast the forward funnel, Burley saw three men desperately hanging on to a rope halfway down the ship's side. It was a hazardous and deteriorating situation with flames above their heads threatening their rope. Burley ordered his men to pull towards them, but even then they argued. Again Burley came up with the appropriate language and again he prevailed. Unfortunately, by the time they neared the ship two of the men had fallen into the sea and were lost. The third, one of the 6-inch gun crew, AB Hamelin, was rescued.

Burley took his boat close in round the bows to the starboard side where he was greeted with cheers. Again it was Delorme's 'curious hilarity'. Whilst Garrett and Pearch must have been very relieved, it is doubtful if *they* felt inclined to cheer.

Garrett took command. As soon as ladders were in position he began herding his survivors downwards. Among them was Mrs Willis.

Mrs Willis had had a miserable time. First she had narrowly missed death on the burning promenade, whence she had been rescued by Ransome and his men. Then she had seen her husband and daughter climb down ropes and swim out to sea in an effort to climb aboard the Captain's boat before it floated away astern. She had no idea what had happened to them and was fearful of the worst.

Now at last her strength failed her and halfway down a rope ladder she let go and plummeted to the water, falling between the lifeboat and the ship's side where she disappeared beneath the surface. It was fortunate that the ubiquitous Garrett saw the incident. An AB Varney was standing by helping people to bridge the gap between the ship's side and the boat. Garrett shouted to him and quickly Varney sized up the situation and dived into the water, found Mrs Willis, pulled her beneath the boat and brought her to the surface. She was quickly pulled aboard. Understandably, she was unconscious.

When Pearch and his deputy went over the side they stopped halfway down to guide a stretcher containing the injured sergeant who had been found by Ransome at the same time as he found Mrs Willis. In the process the Deputy Purser dropped a canvas bag. He yelled—for this bag had other people's money and valuables in it. Another sailor went in after it, caught up with it as it sank and brought it to the surface. One wonders how many people today, looking at a valued piece of jewelry perhaps left to them in somebody's will, realize how nearly they did not get it.

Garrett remained on the forecastle. There were still things to be done and people to be looked after.

* * *

127

George Bonwick had done all he could. He was certain now that the after decks were clear. He was about half a mile from the *Empress*, still gathering in the odd swimmers as they turned up. At one time he hailed a nearby boat asking for assistance with injured passengers. This was Delorme's boat, and some minutes later Delorme entered the sea and swam over. He still had his shoes on.

The shoes were strange. When Delorme went down the rope into the sea he refused to comply with the recommended precaution—'Remove your footwear!' The reason for the instruction is obvious. It relieves the legs of unwanted weight and gives greater facility in treading water and swimming. Delorme says that his deliberate retention of his shoes was simply bravado and he does not applaud his obstinacy. It was a bit silly. He said that if he drowned he would be dead and it would not matter. But if he were rescued and taken ashore he did not want to be seen slapping about the docks in bare feet. A doctor has his dignity, even a pointless one like this.

The time was about 1500.

* * *

Paddling as best they could, Baker and his men in the motor-boat slowly made their way back towards the *Empress*. It was a long, slow haul. By about 1415 they were within half a mile of the ship on its starboard quarter. Here they were at last approached by Commodore Nicholson returning from the *Empress*. Baker explained his difficulties and what he rightly considered the importance of getting his motor-boat to work. The Commodore detailed two engineers who must have been among the survivors from the *Empress* and presumably, but strangely, with tools, and within a short time the engine was giving the odd pop. But that was all. They had to disassemble the petrol line, clean the plugs and points and at last, at about 1430, after a couple of dis-spirited huffs the engine spluttered, halted and then picked up into a steady rhythm. The throttle was opened, the engine raced to warm it up and then she was throttled back to settle into a satisfying roar.

Whilst this was going on, Nicholson had taken the opportunity to transfer an injured man to Baker's boat. Baker then headed for two lifeboats lying stationary. Lines were cast, made fast and very soon the three boats were on their way to the burning forward decks of the *Empress*.

There the situation was grim. The forecastle head, despite the evacuation of some passengers, was still the last resort for many unfortunate people and was crowded to its extremities. The bridge was an incinerated ruin. The forward promenade had disappeared, its stark framework of red-hot metal seen through smoke and flame. Although they could not see it, the forewelldeck, their first refuge, was red hot, buckled and twisted, with such wooden decking as there had been overlaying the steel burned to black ash. Abaft the forewelldeck flames were still roaring up from No 2 hold. There was not much more time.

The wind continued to rise, the earlier swell being whipped up into a cold and choppy sea. Baker dropped his first lifeboat on the starboard bow at about 1500. During the next half hour they embarked about 200 people and when all three boats were loaded they pulled away. Shortly afterwards the engine fluttered, hesitated, popped again and then stopped. They were out of petrol. So much for the state of preparedness in which the boats were said to have been maintained.

Baker's boat slipped the hawsers. It was overcrowded and lay sluggish. An overloaded motor-boat with means of progression is one thing. An overloaded motor-boat without means of progression is something quite different. They began to ship water and set themselves to baling. They turned their bows into the wind and lay there hoping for the best.

* * *

As far as Garrett was concerned, the arrival of the motor-boat with its two pulling boats was the answer to his prayers. Flames were arising from No 1 hatch on the forewelldeck itself. Choking smoke overhung everything.

He was still angry in spite of his relief, but, of course, he did not know the full story. What he did know, or thought he knew, was that Ransome had lost his life because lifeboats had carelessly been allowed to drift. And the 300 or more people on the foreparts of the ship had had their lives placed in jeopardy for the same reason. Many were dead who should not have died.

Garrett, Captain Black, an unnamed sergeant and the ship's

adjutant, Captain Turner, were the last to leave the ship. The inimical forces they left behind were impenetrable smoke, unquenchable flame, exploding .303 ammunition, exploding 6-inch shell fuses, and the tremendous heat from Nos 1 and 2 hatches. All this plus the threat of exploding gas formed in the oil tanks by the excessive heat.

The time was about 1630.

1630: The rescue

Whilst still about 60 miles from the *Empress*, Commander Spurgeon and his officers on *Echo* could already see the smoke rising from her, so great was its volume. They ploughed their way past three trawlers which, with other ships, had been detailed by Flag Officer, Greenock, to proceed to help the stricken ship.

Echo and *Burza* arrived on the scene at 1630. They found lifeboats and rafts scattered over a wide area and riding in a choppy sea, some of them several miles from the *Empress*. As *Echo* approached the area, Commander Spurgeon saw an aircraft hovering over the ship. Again the problem of identification arose and he requested by Aldis lamp that this plane identify itself as friendly by firing a rocket. The plane did this and *Echo* closed and proceeded to pick up survivors from four boats about two miles from the ship. She then closed to within half a mile, continuing to pick up survivors as they came upon them.

Burza's part in the operation was to search out swimming and raft survivors. Amongst these, hanging desperately on to their upturned boat, were those poor, worn-out and bedraggled remnants of Petch and company. Exhausted, half-drowned, clutching at whatever part of the capsized motor-boat they could, they still had the strength and spirit to cheer as *Burza* closed on them and flung scrambling nets over for them to climb. Even so, it was not easy for these poor men to make it up the side of the destroyer. And not all who had set out on their little epic nearly eight bours before did so. Two wounded had been transferred to the Captain's boat. But 12 had gone to their deaths.

The trawlers which the destroyers had passed *en route*

arrived at about 1750. These were the *Drangey*, the *Cape Agona* and the *Paynter*. They proceeded to patrol the area and rescued a further 250 people.

Amongst those rescued by *Echo* were Dr Delorme—still with his shoes on—Fifth Officer George Bonwick and Junior Second Engineer Evans. And, of course, Rona Trotter. Amongst those picked up by the trawlers were the Commodore, the bosun and PO Hitchener. They were on the *Cape Agona*. Later, on Commander Spurgeon's instructions, all survivors on the trawlers were transferred to either *Echo* or *Burza* except for badly injured cases such as two ladies on *Cape Agona* who, at Commodore Nicholson's request, remained on the trawler and were taken to port without being unnecessarily disturbed. They were in the hands of Dr Peake who, it will be remembered, was taken from the sea by Hitchener in No 4 boat. Once recovered from his immersion and exhaustion, he had done a great deal to help others.

CPO Coward was with Major Trotter and the ladies rescued by Chief Steward Moss. They were all taken aboard *Echo* where George Trotter and Rona Trotter must have been very relieved to see one another. One of the odd quirks which arose was that Rona Trotter's husband, Captain Henry Trotter, although hearing about the loss of the *Empress* within a few days, was not to know for several weeks if his wife had survived. One would have thought that the security of the thing would have been more important for the ship than it was for the person, but apparently that was not so. CPO Burley and First Officer Keay also were taken aboard *Echo* after spending some time on *Drangey*.

Captain Sapsworth's lifeboat, as we have seen, was found to have an extraordinary number of ship's officers on board. This was brought to the attention of the Flag Officer in Charge, Greenock, by a personal report from Mr F. Willis, the Naval Stores Officer from Cape Town. Although there is no direct implication of things being wrong, there does seem to be almost half a near hint that such a situation was surprising, when so many passengers had seen so little of the ship's officers during the action. His report says, in part:

'[With] the fire spreading towards us I saw about midships a large lifeboat in which there were a few men with someone in the bows holding onto a long rope attached to the side of the ship ... We all shouted to the lifeboat that there were women and children trapped on the forecastle but the lifeboat appeared to be unable to come up to the forecastle. Suddenly I saw that those in the lifeboat had let go of the rope . . . and the lifeboat began immediately to drift astern . . .

'As this appeared to be the last opportunity of making for a lifeboat my wife and daughter and I agreed that we should swim for this lifeboat which had . . . drifted away from amidships. I then proceeded to swim for the lifeboat followed later by my daughter. After some time I managed to reach the boat completely exhausted but I was dragged on the boat. When I revived I found in the boat the Captain of the ship, the Chief Officer, several junior officers and members of the crew and as far as I could see one passenger. For some reason . . . it was impossible to get the boat up to the ship and having picked up my daughter and some other passengers who had also swum for this boat the Captain ordered the boat to be pulled wherever possible to pick up survivors . . . I estimate we picked up about 25 persons.

'I feel I must add that my wife, who was eventually hauled out of the water by a naval seaman named Varney under the direction of Commander Garrett, RN, OC Naval Draft, informs me that the saving of her life and the lives, she estimates, of about 200 other passengers who were trapped on the forecastle was due entirely to the splendid manner in which Commander Garrett, RN, took charge of the whole forecastle and by his splendid courage and cheerfulness maintained the morale of the passengers concerned and eventually succeeded under the most trying conditions in organizing and controlling the disembarkation of these passengers in the lifeboats which had been collected from various points in the sea and brought alongside by means of the ship's motor-boat . . .'

If this was indeed a sideways attempt to question the actions of the ship's officers by vaguely implying that they had all looked after themselves and that it was a single Royal Navy officer who did their job for them, then the actual story of what happened to these officers individually and the manner in which they came to be in the one boat is a vindication. There was nothing else they could have done but what they did. This is referred to in the Findings of the Board of Enquiry:

'With reference to the report of Mr F. Willis, Naval Stores Officer, attached, we find that the presence of so many executive officers of the ship in the same boat was justified by the fact that while carrying out their duties in lowering the boats they were trapped by the fire and had no alternative but to get into this boat or the water.'

That is fair enough. But to the author, justifiably or otherwise, it is noticeable that throughout Captain Sapsworth's evidence there is to be detected a half sense of personal disquiet which induced an almost unnecessary emphasis on the things he did right; and always a good reason why things which went wrong, did go wrong. There seems to be a self-awareness that maybe he did not do, or could not do, all that he should have done or would have liked to have done, either before the action or during it.

Echo and *Burza* circled the area for some two hours after rescuing all possible survivors, and at the end of this period the destroyers *Broke* and *Sardonyx* arrived. These two ships had been lying at Londonderry at four hours' notice. At 1040 on the 26th they had received orders to raise steam. They had cast off at 1120 and had proceeded at full steam to arrive at the smouldering hulk of the *Empress* at 1850. By this time light was almost gone.

Echo and *Burza* then left for the Clyde, first having given instructions that when possible the *Empress* was to be taken in tow and removed to a home port. *Broke*, *Sardonyx* and the three trawlers were then left to patrol the area. The *Empress* was still burning and must have been completely gutted, with flames still rising from midships sections, whilst the fore and aft sections were still covered in voluminous smoke. Her sides and funnels still appeared to be intact. She had only a slight list to starboard, but her draught was normal and she was lying level, fore and aft, in the water.

* * *

When the survivors were being brought aboard *Echo*, Lieutenant Warrington-Strong, the navigating officer, was off duty from the bridge and therefore was in general charge of the embarkation and welfare of the refugees. The scrambling nets had been lowered over the side and *Echo* was manoeuvred to make a lee for the boats which were rising and falling in the swell. In talks and correspondence, Warrington-Strong has given his impressions of events as he remembers them after more than four decades.

First over the side, being assisted from below, came a young lady, and the sight of her painted fingernails clutching the top rung of the scrambling net seemed to him to be bizarre in the circumstances. It is such small details as this which remain indelibly fixed in Warrington-Strong's mind. The young lady in question was accommodated in the Captain's day cabin together with Lord and Lady Yarborough, as Warrington-Strong had supposed her to be their daughter. In fact, neither of Lord Yarboroughs' two daughters were on the *Empress*, although one of them, now Lady Wendy Lycett, says in a letter, that she heard the story many times from her mother, the late Lady Nancye Yarborough.

The lady with the painted fingernails could have been Mrs Trotter. There were also two Queen Alexandra's Imperial Military Nursing Service sisters placed in the same cabin as Mrs Trotter and Mrs Stephenson, and the painted fingernails could have belonged to any of them except that Mrs (now Lady) Stephenson, in 1989 being 84 years old, would no doubt have been delighted even then at being referred to as a 'young lady'.

However, a photograph owned by Warrington-Strong shows a beautiful young lady wrapped in a blanket smiling unconcernedly as she stands on Gourock pier. As it turns out, according to the *Glasgow Herald*, which owns the original picture, this young lady was Miss Jean Willis, the lady who with her father swam to the Captain's boat, and upon reflection Warrington-Strong believes that she was the lady with the painted fingernails.

The Navigating Officer put his survivors anywhere he could fit them in to make them comfortable, using officers' cabins, the wardroom, every armchair and settee. Bedding was placed in all messdecks and passages. There were a number of wounded and otherwise injured, so the small sick bay and the deck space outside it were crowded. The ship's doctor, assisted by Dr Delorme, Dr Peake and Dr Greig, worked the entire night but was unable to save the lives of two of the most seriously injured. These two men were members of the 3-inch gun crew, injured in the blast when that gun was blown up. They were placed as comfortably as possible, lying face downwards on the deck, their chest injuries being beyond the limited surgical resources available. The ghastly sound of their laboured breathing filled the small space and was most distressing to all concerned. These two men eventually died.

An odd problem then arose, probably due to the fact that none of the ship's crew, as far as is known, had yet taken part in any action resulting in confrontation with the nastiness of death. The question was—where could they put the two corpses?

The facts were that the ship was hurtling along at some 30 knots, through a still dangerous sea, and was overcrowded with refugees cluttering the decks and passages; the only secluded place that seemed to offer itself was the raised gun platform at the after end of the ship. This gun platform was being manned in defence stations by the gun crew of the after 4.7-inch gun—'X' gun. At that degree of readiness this was the only gun out of the total of four which was manned.

The two corpses were wrapped in sheets and placed in wash-deck lockers at the after end of the platform. The steel lids were lowered and all appeared as well as could be expected. But whilst Warrington-Strong was keeping middle watch (midnight to 0400), after having had no sleep, let it be said, for 24 hours, the captain of 'X' gun reported to him on the bridge.

'Beg pardon, Sir, but the gun's crew are rather disturbed by the presence of the corpses and request to keep their watch on "B" gun instead.'

'B' gun was on a raised platform forward of the bridge, and although it was just as effective operationally as 'X' gun, it was exposed to the cold and wet and more often than not drenched with spray. The Officer of the Watch had to call Commander Spurgeon to tell him of this proposed change of armament. Permission was given.

Warrington-Strong and Spurgeon thought it odd even having regard for the inexperience of the gun crew, but it was learned later that as rigor mortis set in, the bodies tended to raise the lids of the lockers as the ship responded to the swell, and the question arose, 'Were those men really dead?' The gunners had tried to weigh down the lids with live shells, but in the end a transfer to 'B' gun seemed expedient.

Another incident in which a badly wounded man died a horrifying death is revealed by Dr Delorme. This was when he had to show Commander Garrett the corpse of one of the gunners. This man was one of those transferred from Petch's boat to the Captain's, severely wounded. He eventually died in the sick bay of the *Echo*. Delorme can not now give a name to this unfortunate man, but since he was one of the naval gunners on the *Empress* and had been wounded in the action, it seems probable that it was AB Andrews. Petch and company had found him at the bottom of a ladder, had hoisted him by rope to the boat deck, placed him in the motor-boat and had succoured him until the Captain's boat took him.

He had remained alive throughout all those horrifying hours and had succumbed inevitably because, as Delorme showed Garrett, he had sustained severe brain and facial injuries. Garrett had blanched when he saw the man and told Delorme he hoped never to see anything as gruesome again. It was, as we have said, early on in the war.

Dr Delorme also tells the story of Stanley Keay, the First Officer. He was another brave man. With CPO Burley he had been in charge of the lifeboat which collided with the motor-boat and had handed over command to Burley when he realized he was too injured to carry on himself. Delorme says:

'Stanley Keay had become a good friend of mine during my year on the ship. His story is a good one although I didn't get it until later on board *Echo*. He was on the bridge with Captain Sapsworth when the attack began and he was blown down a companion-way by a blast, smashing his arm. He kept this a secret from me until I had dealt with all the other casualties, and this was not until the following day. By that time his forearm was badly swollen and later he developed Volkmann's ischaemic paralysis.'

In fact, it is difficult to see how Mr Keay could have suffered this injury whilst he was on the bridge with the Captain, for although he was senior officer of the watch, Sapsworth had relieved him when the first bomb fell. Keay had then gone down to where Second Officer Stanley had met him with the carpenter's mate on the starboard side of the Mall. There is no mention of injury then, and the First Officer seemed to be carrying on normally. Mr Stanley had accompanied Mr Keay and the carpenter to the promenade deck and they had connected up two hoses. Still no mention of injury. Then Stanley had gone down to 'B' deck, where his fire party should have been, but returned to the promenade 10 minutes later where he again met Mr Keay and Keay told him he was going to see the Captain to tell him how bad the situation was. Keay had then departed for the bridge. Still no mention of injury.

If he received the injury whilst returning to the bridge, it must have been about 0950 when the last bomb fell. But that bomb, if there was only one, fell just forward of and under the docking bridge and abaft the after funnel, nearly 500 feet abaft the bridge. How could it have knocked Mr Keay off the bridge companion-way at that distance, with so much ship's super-structure and three funnels between?

It is more probable that he hurt his arm during the collision between the motor-boat and the lifeboat, for just before that CPO Burley said Mr Keay came down a rope into his boat. How could he have done that with only one good arm? It was after the collison that Burley said, 'Mr Keay had hurt his arm.'

But it does not matter. Mr Keay was a brave and unassuming man who had taken charge of a lifeboat under extremely difficult conditions and with Burley's help had brought it back to the ship against the protests of less worthy men. Despite what must have been excruciating pain, he made no complaint until next day when, after his friend Eddy Delorme had seen to everyone else, he then allowed his wound to be attended to.

It is a pity that he was so brave because otherwise something might have been done to save him from what became a life-long disability. For Mr Keay lived the remainder of his life with a withered arm. Despite this he was to live to command several Canadian Pacific ships, one of them being a new, but smaller, *Empress of Britain*.

Dr Delorme also treated the Chief Officer, Mr Davies, whilst on *Echo*. Delorme says Davies was injured by multiple small fragments of metal from an incendiary. Although the wounds did not appear to be serious and ... 'Mr Davies seemed all right' ... he was to spend a long time in hospital due to complications in what were 'relatively superficial wounds'.

This again is something of a mystery. Apart from a short time after the first attack, the Chief Officer had been on the bridge with the Captain and had left when the Captain left. This is what Sapsworth said. Bernard Jope was to say that he carried no incendiary bombs and that all the bombs which hit fell abaft the centre funnel, one of them almost at the stern. There was the whole of the bridge superstructure and at least one huge funnel between the bomb strikes and the Chief Officer. How could he have been hit by incendiary fragments or, for that matter, any other bomb fragments? It is more probable that his wounds were from cannon fire, although in that case they would hardly have been fragmentation wounds. Splinters from the steel superstructure, perhaps? Still, again, it does not really matter.

It might have helped to solve these minor discrepancies if both or either the First Officer and the Chief Officer had been able to give evidence at the Board of Enquiry, but both of them were in hospital. By the same token it would have been interesting and indeed proper for Dr Delorme to have given evidence, not only for the purpose of correcting any minor discrepancies about a number of factors, but also to express opinions on the future disposition of medical facilities, casualty stations and equipment on lifeboats. Further again, there is no doubt that had the doctor been there to give evidence, he would have made sure that the bravery of poor Jimmy England was recognized. In view of the awards which were made as a result of this action, it is surprising that it was not recognized.

But the fact of the matter was that immediately upon landing at Gourock, Delorme took steps to join the RNVR and was sent helter-skelter to Chatham. Subsequently he spent most of the war with submarines and submariners, amongst them being the Victoria Cross winners, Godfrey Place and Donald Cameron.

Apart from the affair of the badly injured, perhaps one of the most poignant episodes on the *Echo* experienced by Dr Delorme was his meeting with Captain Sapsworth. Delorme assisted and was assisted by *Echo*'s own doctor, and they worked ceaselessly for many hours amongst the injured, the dying and the dead. There was no respite until the early hours of the morning. They carried on with their desperate work without interruption.

But just before dawn, after everything that could be done had been done, Captain Sapsworth sent for Delorme and asked for a report. The doctor found him sitting alone. He was tired to the point of utter exhaustion, and deeply sorrowful for the loss of life which might not have occurred had circumstances not been so dead set against him. And he was a picture of utter despair at the loss of his ship. Dr Delorme says:

'God knows, it wasn't his fault. As for his leaving the ship too soon [as had been implied by rumours and other sources] anyone who saw the fires that seemed to creep forward faster than aft would not expect anyone to remain and be barbecued . . .'

He goes on to say, typical of this gentleman:

'I have not the slightest doubt that all the deck officers including the Captain acted with their normal resolution and discipline. Mr Davies, the Chief Officer, told me that when the ship was attacked, Captain Sapsworth stood by the Lewis gunners on the bridge giving them all his encouragement.'

Lieutenant Commander Garrett and his companions were eventually picked up, some by *Echo*, some by *Burza* and some by the trawlers; those on the trawlers were later transferred to the destroyers. At Greenock, Garrett states that he ensured that all wounded and dead on *Echo* were sent to the hospital in charge of the Captain in Charge, Greenock. He did the same for those on *Burza*. He then took the remainder of this draft to Glasgow where the naval authorities 'very kindly did everything they could for my men and we eventually dispersed to our naval ports.'

A job well done.

And so, apart from the Board of Enquiry at St Enoch Hotel in Glasgow on 29 October 1940, the affair was finished so far as those who had been on board the *Empress of Britain* were concerned.

But the *Empress* lived on for two more days before the final action which destroyed her.

2

Sunday, 27 October 1940: the tow

Echo and *Burza* departed the scene upon the arrival of *Broke* and *Sardonyx*. Before doing so, Captain Sapsworth and Commander Spurgeon had consulted and concluded that since the fire appeared to be dying down and the *Empress* was still afloat with her draught normal—although the midships section was still flaming and there was a lot of smoke fore and aft—it would be possible for her to be towed to the Clyde under escort.

This was signalled to the Flag Officer in Charge, Greenock, and the Commanders of *Broke* and *Sardonyx* were so instructed. *Broke*'s Commander concurred, but considered that even though the situation was improving it would be unlikely that boarding could take place for at least 24 hours. *Broke* and *Sardonyx* then proceeded to carry out an asdic sweep until daylight on the 27th.

The Commander of *Broke* then considered the situation of the trawlers which, extraordinarily enough for the job they had done, were no less than nine days out from port and their fuel supply was getting low. They were, unfortunately, as it turned out, ordered to proceed to Belfast. *Broke*'s Commander was later forced to realize that the relief of the trawlers without replacement was premature and indeed a grave mistake because it greatly reduced the capacity to escort the vulnerable *Empress* whilst she was proceeding to port under tow. The escort was now left entirely to the two destroyers.

In any event, the arrival of HM Tugs *Marauder* and *Thames* was expected and the towing job would be theirs, not that they would be able to help much in the matter of escorting their charge. The record does not say where the two tugs were when they were ordered to proceed to assist the *Empress*, but it does say that by 1540 hours on the 26th they were off Inishtrahull lighthouse, about 10 miles north of the west Irish coast and proceeding at a top speed of 14 knots. They arrived at daybreak. The *Empress* was still burning.

In the meantime, HMS *Cairo* had arrived. She turned up at 0040 and immediately ordered *Broke* to screen her and *Sardonyx* as they circled the wreck. At 0559 *Cairo* was instructed by FOIC Greenock to return to harbour and to leave *Broke* in charge.

Although by daybreak it was observed that the *Empress* was still on fire, the smoke had diminished and it seemed possible that a boarding party might go aboard her sooner than had previously been thought. The decision was made despite *Broke*'s Commander's own words: 'There were flames in the forewelldeck, smoke rising from ventilators on the forecastle head and the stability of the foremast doubtful'.

In the meantime, HM Tug *Seaman* was also now on its way. *Seaman* had been berthed at Londonderry like *Broke* and *Sardonyx* when she received orders at 1045 from FOIC through NOIC Londonderry to proceed to the *Empress*. She left her berth at 1200. The weather was fine and clear and there was a slight north-westerly breeze.

At 1510 she received a corrected position by radio—the *Empress* had drifted. She drifted again in the course of the night and a further new position was given to *Seaman* at 0340 on the 27th. *Seaman* had arrived on the scene by 0900 on the 27th. The *Empress* was still burning.

At 1030 *Broke* informed *Seaman* that *Thames* would connect on the port bow and *Marauder* on the starboard bow. *Seaman* would just have to get in where she could, but the only possible position left was between the two higher-powered tugs. But this was not practical because it would mean that *Thames* and *Marauder* would have to reduce their speed to allow *Seaman* to keep her position, and this would mean the slowing down of an already dangerously slow tow. The fact was that *Seaman* was more an encumbrance than she was a help, and at 1200, after standing by for an hour, she was ordered back to port by *Broke*.

The motor-boat from *Broke* had been lowered at 0930 and 16

men under command of Sub-Lieutenant Angus Letty DSC RNR boarded the *Empress* using a Jacob's ladder which Garrett had left hanging from the forecastle rail. Letty and his men found the *Empress* gutted and some parts still aflame. Hatches were wide open, booms had collapsed, steel decks were distorted, some of them still red-hot; there was broken glass everywhere, and some pathetic-looking improvised rafts, some of them burned, lay littering the deck with other miscellaneous debris. It was a scene of the utmost desolation and a grim mockery of the epitome of luxury she had been but a few hours before.

The boarding party proceeded to secure hawsers from the two tugs, and by 1050 they had left the wreck, taking with them some personal effects and a quantity of money. These were, in accordance with normal procedure, eventually handed over to the Receiver of Wrecks. The party was back on board *Broke* by 1100 and shortly after that the tow started.

The speed of the tow settled down to a steady four knots with the two destroyers carrying out asdic sweeps on both sides, *Broke* proceeding at 15 knots and *Sardonyx*, because of her lesser fuel reserves and the need to conserve, at 12 knots.

Before *Seaman* left she was instructed to collect as many lifeboats as she could and tow them back to Londonderry. By 1300 she had found eight and one motor-boat, but the tow was a failure. By 1700 five of the boats had become waterlogged despite a slow towing speed, and they sank. At 2400 the motor-boat came apart, the forward end breaking off completely, and she also sank. Two other lifeboats followed suit in rapid succession. At about this time *Seaman* passed through some miscellaneous wreckage and amongst this she found one more lifeboat and took it in tow.

Seaman's Commander commented that these boats were very frail, being made of plywood. One wonders why. Surely a sea-going liner deserved better security for her high-price-paying passengers than 'frail' plywood. In the author's recollection, by far the greater majority of lifeboats he ever saw were made of sturdy steel. Maybe there was, after all, more 'cosmetic' about the glamorous *Empress* than was visible to any but the aware and discerning eye.

Seaman reached port with only one lifeboat.

* * *

Three things of significance occurred between Letty's boarding of the *Empress* and 1230. The first was the dramatic but brief appearance of a German plane—another FW Condor in fact—which stayed only long enough to observe what was going on. Shortly afterwards the second significant thing took place.

A Whitley heavy bomber of Coastal Command reported that she had sighted a U-boat heading north towards the position of the *Empress*. The report did not say whether she had attacked the U-boat, which is surprising, for it might have helped to the extent of making the U-boat dive deep, change course and slow down. But there it was—56 miles to the south and, according to the pilot, proceeding under water. Was this the reason why the Whitley didn't attack? But it is unlikely that the U-boat was under water for with choppy seas the Whitley would indeed have been lucky to have spotted a submarine below the surface.

It may be considered that the Condor, having noted that steps were being taken to salvage the *Empress*, radioed Berlin and Berlin in its turn informed the Commander of the U-boat, Oberleutnant Hans Jenisch. He was later to say that whilst he had seen the Condor, no communication had taken place between them. He was also to say, contrary to the Whitley report, that he was travelling on the surface for maximum speed.

The third item of significance was that it was the tug *Marauder* which, at 1230, reported by radio to FOIC Greenock that she and *Thames* had the *Empress* in tow and were proceeding at five knots. One would have supposed that the authority for this report would have been the warship in charge of the operation, *Broke*. And this apparent attitude of the Commander of *Marauder* to go over the head of *Broke*, or even to ignore her, is discernible in some of the events which followed.

As a result of the appearance of the Condor and the report about the U-boat, *Broke* ordered *Sardonyx* to sweep, keeping astern of the beam of the tugs, and to remain within sight and easy reach of the *Empress*. The Commander reasonably expected that should there be an attack it would be during the night—the U-boat had at least seven hours to travel—and would be from astern. *Broke* herself continued to sweep astern. The position at dusk—about 1850—was 55° 06 north and 10° 37 west. The convoy's course was 070°, its speed being maintained at about four knots, and the weather conditions were good.

Nothing untoward happened during the remainder of that day. But something untoward *was* to happen in the early hours of the following morning, 28th October.

* * *

The German U-boat *U32* commanded by Oberleutnant Hans Jenisch was one of the only two U-boats at sea at that date. She had left the new German base at Lorient in Brittany in the early hours of 24 October, and had headed west. Late in the evening of the 26th, Jenisch had picked up a dramatic radio broadcast from Berlin telling of the action against *Empress of Britain* and claiming complete destruction of this most important vessel. The claim of 'complete destruction' was premature, as we know, because the *Empress* lived on and was salvagable for 40 hours after the Condor's first attack.

Later that evening, whilst Jenisch had been patrolling an area about 60 miles south-west of the *Empress*, he received an official message confirming that the ship had been attacked by aircraft and was now a blazing wreck, abandoned and adrift. There were several reasons why Jenisch did not immediately head towards her. Four reasons, in fact. One—if the *Empress* was completely destroyed there was little point in attacking her again, especially in an area which was bound to be thick with enemy warships and planes. Two—he was given no direct order to do so. Three—he had been informed of a convoy somewhere in the area. This could have been either the *Ettrick/Kranga/Escapade/Echo/Burza/Blyskawica* convoy from which *Echo* and *Burza* had detached to go to the aid of the *Empress*, or another convoy still lying to the south and west which later was to come into the picture—Convoy SC8. The fourth reason was simply that he was under the impression that the only other U-boat at sea, *U31*, was much nearer the *Empress* than he was. He therefore took no action.

But early in the morning of the 27th the message was repeated with the added information that the *Empress* was still afloat, on an even keel, and her draught showed no signs that she was holed or likely to sink. Further, British activities indicated that she would be taken in tow and hauled to a British port—after all, not so very far away—where she could be succoured, refurbished and sent to sea again as important as ever to the British in the war at sea. In which case this German success would turn out to be a hollow one.

Jenisch decided to intercept her with all dispatch. He needed as much speed as possible and so travelled on the surface. Late in the forenoon he was close enough to see the ship's masts, but shortly after was forced to submerge in a hurry by the arrival of a patrolling Sunderland.

He remained submerged for the remainder of the day, but observed the activities of the destroyers. He was astern of the convoy and was able to maintain a speed submerged which enabled him to keep up with it. 'Hiding in its wake,' as Jenisch put it.

The screening destroyers maintained a zig-zag pattern with *Sardonyx* mainly to port of the *Empress* and *Broke* astern and to starboard. One can see now why *Broke*'s Commander wished he had not let the anti-submarine trawlers go back to port, for they could most effectively have filled in the gaps abreast of the ship on both sides.

Jenisch remained submerged till dusk. When he surfaced he was unable to see the target. He carried out a comprehensive search for some hours but had no luck. He submerged again. Shortly afterwards his underwater detecting device picked up the sounds of a ship's engines and he was able to locate their position a few miles to the east. He proceeded towards them and by midnight he had the *Empress* and her escort in sight. The engines he had heard were those of the tugs and destroyers. He observed that the convoy was still travelling at about four knots and, submerged, he could still trail it with ease. From his position astern of it he worked out the pattern of the escort and in time found a gap. He then slipped inside the screen.

3

Monday, 28 October 1940: the sinking

From this point it is difficult to tie up events and times in *Broke*'s report with that of either Jenisch or that ascribed to *Sardonyx*. The times and sequence of events appear to be out of kilter. It is a great pity that *Sardonyx*'s report on the action has disappeared and cannot be used to check and clarify anomalous details. All the author can do is first of all to give Jenisch's version (which cannot now be checked by personal contact, for Jenisch died at the very time a letter from the author was on its way to him) and then repeat verbatim the relevant parts of *Broke*'s report.

U32 surfaced at about 0150. She was about 500 metres from and slightly ahead of the *Empress*, inside the destroyers screen and not very far from *Sardonyx*. At 0200 she fired two torpedoes. The first of these malfunctioned—a common occurence at this stage of the war, according to the writer, Len Deighton (*Blitzkrieg*)—exploded prematurely and her presence was betrayed. The second presumably missed its target, because it is not recorded as a hit. Jenisch immediately fired a third torpedo and this hit amidships. The time must have been about 0205. Jenisch noted that immediately after the hit a great mushroom of steam arose and he concluded that a boiler had burst. Oddly, he also says that immediately after the premature explosion he saw lights moving on the ship, star shells and flares going up and he also heard sirens. All of these are highly likely with the exception of the lights moving on the ship, for there was no one on board.

Immediately after the strike Jenisch simply took his U-Boat astern of its victim and, remaining on the surface, awaited events. Whilst there a Sunderland flew over him once again, and again did not see him. But his stay was brief because 9 minutes after the explosion *Empress of Britain* heeled slowly over to port and sank. *U32* dropped astern and disappeared from the picture—but only for two days, because on 30 October, as we shall see, retribution caught up with her.

* * *

The relevant parts of *Broke*'s report are repeated word for word as they were written because that will eliminate any temptation to improvise to make things fit—which they do not quite do.

EXTRACT FROM REPORT BY COMMANDER OF HMS BROKE—29/10/40

9. At 0145 *Broke* was about two miles on the starboard quarter of the *Empress of Britain* and was just turning to start a zig-zag up the starboard side. *Sardonyx* was six cables from the liner on her port quarter steering 050°. At this moment two explosions were heard, which I took to be depth charges, and shortly after a red Very light was seen from *Sardonyx* indicating that an attack had been made. Three gun flashes were also seen. I steered at once to close *Sardonyx* on the assumption that she had dropped depth charges on a contact. *Sardonyx* was heard trying to communicate in 1579 k/cs but was jammed by 'Whitehall'; *Broke*'s R/T was unfortunately out of action. The visibility was variable owing to passing rain showers and there was no moon.

10. While still trying to locate *Sardonyx*'s contact, at 0230 flashing was seen from the expected bearing of *Marauder*. I thought she was doing this to indicate her position and considered it more important to join *Sardonyx*. Eventually, *Broke*, not having had a contact, was signalled by *Sardonyx* that she had lost contact and had no reason to suppose she had been in contact with a submarine. Accordingly both ships set out to sweep back towards the convoy. At 0440 I left *Sardonyx* in order to investigate a light which turned out to be a steam fishing trawler.

11. From 0530 until daylight I tried to find the tugs and their tow but it was not until 0940 that I met *Sardonyx*. I then heard for the first time that the *Empress of Britain* had sunk about nine minutes after the explosions.

12. *Sardonyx* signalled that a bright flash had been seen abreast the bridge and two explosions had been felt, that the liner had been seen to list heavily to port and sink about nine minutes later. She stated also that she had seen the tugs after their tow had sunk.

13. I was anxious about the tugs and we turned back to the position of the sinking to search for them. The *Marauder* was called in 1579 and 1500 k/cs but without result. At the same time I reported (by signal 1025/28) what had happened.

14. *Broke* and *Sardonyx* continued to sweep in the neighbourhood of the wreck until ordered to return to Londonderry (C in C 1757/28).

15. Until the announcement in the German wireless news there was no evidence to show what caused the explosions. An attack was expected by both destroyers by the U-boat referred to in paragraph 8 above (the one reported by the Whitley). In the *Sardonyx* a midshipman asleep in the wardroom was woken up by what he took to be the noise of the discharge of torpedoes and arrived on the bridge in time for the explosions. The officer of the watch also reported to the Captain an unusual pulsation of the ship about five minutes before the explosions. I personally felt at the time and during the following day that an oil fuel explosion was just as likely to have been the cause. The ship was a shell full of incandescent matter and oil fuel left in her tanks must have been in a highly inflammable state. An increase in the flames and smoke near the bridge was noted by *Sardonyx* at 0100 hours.

The report goes on to give reasons why the screening of such a target as was presented by the *Empress of Britain* had been difficult.

* * *

If the above report appears a little subjective and uncertain, it must be remembered that *Broke*'s Commander, once having let the trawlers go, was presented with a most difficult task with a huge area to screen, complicated by the fact that the convoy could only travel at four knots, a speed which would have been ideal for an attacking U-boat to manoeuvre itself into an advantageous position. If his situation had been anything like that of Commander Spurgeon in *Echo* as regards junior officers, he also would have been 'watch-on-stop-on' and very short of sleep. On the other hand he had been at sea less than 48 hours.

Some elements of the situation are worthy of further comment. In the absence of a report from *Sardonyx* (it has disappeared into history) we do not even know if she really fired any depth charges. She herself does not appear to have said so (although she fired a red Very light indicating that an attack had been made—according to *Broke* at about 0145) and Jenisch made no mention of being attacked. If there were depth charges fired at that time in a pattern to encompass a target, ie the source of an asdic contact, then Jenisch would at least have been aware of them, even though he was on the surface.

The star shells, the flares and the sirens Jenisch says he saw and heard are highly probable, since immediately upon the premature explosion almost certainly *Sardonyx* and the two tugs would have fired star shells to see what was going on and would have sounded their sirens to alert one another and *Broke*.

The lights Jenisch says he saw on the *Empress* are another matter because as far as anyone knew there was no one on board. There is no mention of any personnel being left there after Sub-Lieutenant Letty left during the morning of the 27th. Once they had made the hawsers fast there would have been no need, and in any case it would have been an unnecessary hazard with the fires still burning and the ever-present possibility of an all-destroying explosion.

It has been suggested that the tug commanders themselves put men on board to tend the hawsers, but this is highly unlikely without *Broke*'s Commander knowing about it. And if they were there, what happened to them? On the other hand, strangely enough as we shall see, the tug commanders did not seem very concerned about keeping the convoy commander informed about anything.

In any case, since as it turns out the hawsers, as expected, were slipped by the tugs and not by the tow when the *Empress* sank, the likelihood of anyone being on board at the time may be discounted and the lights seen, or thought to have been seen, by Jenisch remain a mystery—except that they could have been just flaring up of fires on the *Empress*. An increase in flame had been noted by *Sardonyx* on the bridge at 0100 and this had probably been due to the strengthening easterly wind into which the ill-fated vessel was heading.

But what about the explosions *Broke* heard at 0145? At that time no torpedoes had been fired, so they cannot have been the cause. If depth charges had been fired, how was it possible for Jenisch not to have noticed them? Could it be that *Broke* mistook the time and the explosions she heard *were* the torpedoes?

Suppose *Sardonyx* had attacked by depth charge. The U-boat was on the surface and would not have been the contact. What would the target have been? *Sardonyx* was later to say that her contact had been lost and there was no reason to suppose that it had been a submarine. Did she then see something on the surface and open fire at it with her guns—and was it this firing that *Broke* heard?

Broke says she saw three gun flashes, but they remain unexplained unless *Sardonyx* did indeed fire them. But again, if this is so, why did *Sardonyx* not say so, thus explaining her red Very light, instead of just casually saying that her sub-surface asdic contact may not have been a submarine?

Broke says she did not know about the *Empress* sinking until she sighted *Sardonyx* at 0940 on the 28th. But her report goes on to say that '*Sardonyx* signalled that a bright flash had been seen abreast of the bridge and two explosions felt, that the liner had been seen to list heavily to port and sink nine minutes later'.

But if *Sardonyx* saw this happening, why did she not tell *Broke* before? They had been in contact for some hours before 0940 for, *Broke* says, 'I left *Sardonyx* at 0440 to investigate a light which turned out to be a steam trawler'. This was 2½ hours after the *Empress* sank.

It is odd, to say the least of it.

Another of the odd things about the towing operation was the apparent lack of cooperation and communication between the tugs and the destroyers. It is quite apparent that *Broke* made every possible effort to watch over the tugs, but as far as can be seen the tugs did not reciprocate in any way. It seems almost as though the Commander of *Marauder* had a bit of a chip on his shoulder about the Royal Navy. Such a situation between auxiliary naval craft and the *real* Royal Navy was not unheard of. Indeed, the author himself (who incidentally was neither Royal Navy nor Merchant Navy) can recall a case in which the master of a tug obstinately refused to pull alongside a very, very much larger RN vessel with the dogmatic comment, '—him. Let him pull alongside me.'

The first example of *Marauder*'s attitude was when she herself reported to Flag Officer in Charge, Greenock, that she had the *Empress* in tow, instead of reporting to *Broke* which was in charge of the operation, so that she could make the report. During the tow, neither *Marauder* nor *Thames* contacted *Broke* or, as far as is known, *Sardonyx*, the only sign of any signal being the flashing light which *Broke* had assumed to be *Marauder* indicating her position and which she had not investigated. No explanation of the flashing light was ever given.

After the sighting of the tugs by *Sardonyx* shortly after the sinking, nothing more was seen of them. It was *Marauder* which initially reported the loss to FOIC Greenock, again going over the head of *Broke*. Then, apparently, the two tugs just went off home without bothering to tell either of the destroyers, which then spent several hours looking for them. They made no attempt to contact them by radio or any other means, neither did they bother to reply to or acknowledge *Broke*'s attempts to communicate with them. And when it came to the Board of Enquiry which was to follow, neither of the two tug commanders made themselves available to give evidence.

4

Wednesday, 30 October 1940: the duel

One might have supposed that with the final sinking of the *Empress of Britain* and the departure of the rescue and escorting vessels, the story had ended. But it had not.

In the forenoon of 30 October, 1940, HMS *Harvester*, commanded by Commander Mark Thornton, had been rounding up stragglers of Convoy SC8. Having tracked them down and established that nothing untoward had happened to them, he gave each a course for the convoy and sent them on their way towards Clyde. *Harvester* then sought out the Commodore of the convoy. There is no record of his name or that of his ship, but *Harvester* found him at 1230 and was informed that one ship was unaccounted for. This was SS *Balzac*, a smallish 5000-ton slow-moving freighter. *Harvester* set out to find her.

Thirteen minutes later, at 1243, *Harvester* picked up a distress signal from *Balzac* saying that she had been attacked by shelling. She was then heading east at top speed. She gave her position as 55°.38 north and 12°.15 west. She was about 80 miles north of *Harvester*.

In the meantime, HMS *Highlander* (Commander William Dallmeyer) had also picked up *Balzac*'s signal. *Balzac* was 45 miles from *Highlander* on a bearing of 270°. *Highlander* also set off to find her. *Harvester* swept from the south and *Highlander* from the east, and at 1617 the two warships met in the position they had expected to find *Balzac*. Neither of the two destroyers had at that time picked up any asdic contact which could be classified as a submarine.

The two ships exchanged signals and shortly *Harvester* was ordered to detach and head for the Clyde, assuming her original role as escort for Convoy SC8. She set a course of 052° and moved off at 25 knots.

She met *Balzac* about 40 miles to the east. The time was 1753. She closed her and interrogated her about the morning's attack. *Balzac* had seen no torpedo track but a huge explosion had occurred at 1142 on her port quarter about 50 yards off, which her Master had taken for a bursting shell. No adversary was seen. The Master had simply headed east at top speed, hoping to catch up with the convoy and, later in the day, and not finding it, had adopted a zig-zag pattern as a safety measure. And nothing further untoward had happened. *Harvester* signalled to this effect to *Highlander* which was then about 10 miles away.

Considering that the U-boat—for so the aggressor was assumed to be—having missed with its first shot would not be happy to allow a solitary ship to escape, *Harvester* concluded that it would not be very far away. She dropped her speed to 15 knots and began anti-submarine operations. She zig-zagged the area, sweeping from *Balzac*'s starboard quarter to her port bow. She made her first contact at 1812.

This was at very short range, when *Harvester* was about 1,000 yards from *Balzac*'s bow. The contact having been made, visual watch was intensified and almost immediately the lookout saw a periscope emerge about two feet out of the water about 150 yards away. Commander Thornton regarded this as a heaven-sent opportunity to ram. Damn it—the U-boat was almost under his feet!

He snapped out his orders.

'Full astern port! Full ahead starboard! Hard aport!'

This would bring *Harvester* round with almost shattering swiftness and if the U-boat had been slower—she was doing about nine knots at the time—*Harvester* would have cracked her in half. As it was, the U-boat's speed enabled her to pass outside *Harvester*'s turning circle and the destroyer passed across the U-boat's stern, missing by yards.

Realizing what had happened, Thornton reversed his engines, now ordering full ahead port and full astern starboard and hard to starboard on the wheel, to bring his ship swinging round sharply. The violent fluctuations on the engines and wheel stunned *Harvester* almost to a dead stop. The U-boat submerged in a great hurry.

Harvester picked up and continued on her course like a greyhound that had just missed a hare, with Thornton left in something of a dilemma. For if the U-boat now turned to starboard, that is towards *Balzac*, obviously Thornton could not fire his pattern of depth charges in the direction of the U-boat without threatening *Balzac*. But if the U-boat turned to port then it would run smack into anything *Harvester* dropped and that almost certainly would mean disaster for her. But in any case, Thornton reasoned, even if the U-boat did escape by steering towards *Balzac*, it was still likely that the shock of a six charge pattern would be severe enough if not to damage the U-boat, then at least to upset the morale of her crew. He fired his six charge pattern. The U-boat steered to starboard and for the time being escaped.

Harvester continued on, turning at a thousand yards and circling to starboard. Almost immediately she picked up a further contact. The time was 1838.

By 1840 *Highlander* had arrived on the scene and was closing. *Harvester* signalled the range and bearing of her contact. Unfortunately *Balzac* was still in the way almost dead in line with *Highlander*'s approach, impeding her attack. *Highlander* signalled her urgently saying she was standing in to danger, telling her to get out of the way and giving her a course to the south-west which would take her clear.

At 1843 *Harvester* again lost her contact, probably because the U-boat was now end-on. Almost immediately she got another. This was quickly classified as non-sub. Goodness knows what it was. In the meantime, *Highlander* was closing and *Balzac* was steering to starboard and away from the area of suspected danger. The U-boat was obviously trying to stick to her to avoid another depth charge attack. But *Highlander* now had a good contact, dropped a calcium flare over the position and signalled the range and bearing to *Harvester*, looking for confirmation. *Balzac* pulled away quickly to starboard.

The original intention here was that if *Harvester* confirmed the contact, *Highlander* would attack. As it happened, *Harvester* did get a contact at 1850 but for some reason there was delay in confirming. *Highlander* did not mess about. She considered that both destroyers were in ideal positions, she as attacker and *Harvester* as director, and it would be criminal to

Not to scale

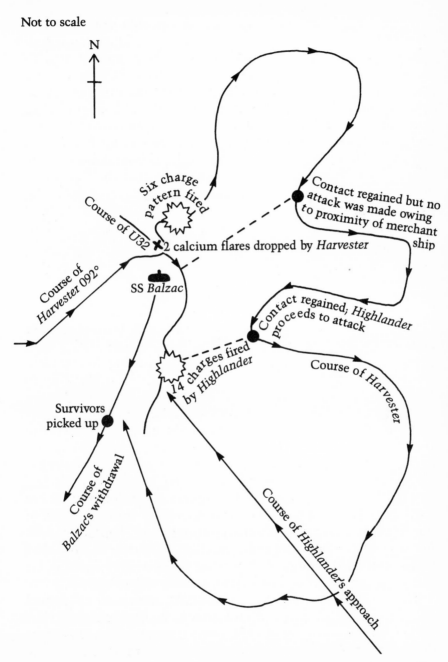

N

Six charge pattern fired

Course of U32

Contact regained but no attack was made owing to proximity of merchant ship

2 calcium flares dropped by *Harvester*

Course of *Harvester* 092°

SS *Balzac*

Contact regained; Highlander proceeds to attack

14 charges fired by Highlander

Course of *Harvester*

Survivors picked up

Course of *Balzac's* withdrawal

Course of *Highlander's* approach

HMS Harvester's *plan of action against* U32. *(*PRO, Kew, and Controller of HM Stationery Office; ADM 199/121, p108*)*

miss the opportunity. She took *Harvester*'s confirmation for granted and moved in from the south at 18 knots. *Harvester* was coming in at a similar speed and at right angles to *Highlander*'s track, and for one horrible moment it seemed that there might be one awful cock-up, to use an expression of the times, and they would collide. *Harvester* gave way, reversed her engines, steered to port, but held on to her contact.

Highlander went in and fired a pattern of 14 depth charges onto the position indicated by the plot and contact. Immediately *Harvester*'s contact dissolved into a messy confusion of echoes and was lost.

At 1856 *Harvester* turned into a near parallel course to *Highlander* so that both vessels were ready to sweep if the attack had failed. At 1903 *Highlander* turned to starboard and regained her contact. At 1904 large air bubbles were seen on *Highlander*'s starboard quarter. At 1907 she observed a track on her port bow and moved to investigate it, thinking it could be a periscope or even a conning tower. She prepared to ram. She quickly discovered that the single track was, in fact, two tracks, and they were torpedoes—*going nowhere!*

Within seconds there was a gigantic thrusting aside of water and up came the U-boat at extremely high speed. Her bows stood clear of the water at an angle of 30 degrees, her stern well down, torpedo tubes showing. Obviously she was badly damaged.

Highlander opened up at point blank range with her 4.7-inch guns, at the same time signalling *Harvester* that the U-boat had surfaced. The light was almost gone and *Highlander* could not see the effect of her attack except that there was one certain hit on the conning tower.

There was now the probability of the crew abandoning and taking to the water. If they did this it would mean they had scuttled. But Dallmeyer was thinking in terms of capturing the vessel, so he opened fire with his .5 machine-guns in an attempt to keep the German crew below decks. If he could keep them there they could not scuttle unless they wanted to commit suicide. It was an interesting thought. But unfortunately for Dallmeyer, the Germans had moved too quickly and the crew was already entering the water. The seacocks had been opened.

* * *

But what happened on board *U32*? Hans Jenisch died in 1982, so whilst we have first-hand German-side information from Bernard Jope about the Condor attack, we have to do without similar information concerning the U-boat. Fortunately, the story was told to others before Jenisch died, both whilst he was attending a course with the Royal Navy in Portsmouth in 1964 and also during annual U32 reunions attended by Mark Thornton, where the latter was toasted by the Germans with a silver cup. On Thornton's death, the Germans presented this cup to his son, James Thornton.

Jenisch had remained with the German Navy after the war and had served as West German Naval Representative at NATO. Whilst there, he had told his story of what happened on board *U32* during the action on several occasions.

Early in the forenoon of 30 October, 1940, just two days after the destruction of the *Empress of Britain*, U32 was patrolling on the surface in the general area of 55° north and 12° west, approximately 200 miles west of Inishtrahull lighthouse. Since her success in sinking the famous liner, nothing exciting had happened. She had been at sea for nearly seven days having left Lorient in the cold, grey dawn of the 24th.

Then she received information of a British convoy heading towards the Clyde. This was Convoy SC8, probably on its way from the Cape. If it had been coming from that other great convoy marshalling point, Halifax, Nova Scotia, her escort would hardly have been rounding up stragglers to the south— but there is today no information available.

Jenisch headed at top speed towards the estimated position. He reached it at 1130 and found only one ship, a small freighter called *Balzac*. He approached his victim on her port quarter, which was apparently the normal manner of approaching a small ship because if she were armed she would hardly be sturdy enough to mount a large naval gun on her stern, and such guns as she had would be mounted forward on the forecastle. With large ships, armed usually with heavy 6-inch naval guns, the situation was different, as with the *Empress* for example, for this armament was mounted at the stern, rendering it expedient for attacking U-boats to approach either from a forward position or on the beam.

The trouble was that in this case, being astern and on the quarter, with a top underwater speed unable to match even that of a medium-speed freighter, Jenisch had to hit with his first shot. If he missed, the ship would simply take off at full speed away from him and he would not get a second chance. He could, of course, fire two or more torpedoes in quick succession, although he might first wait to establish that his first shot had missed. No good wasting torpedoes. If it had been a larger or more important target, he would almost certainly have fired two shots at the outset.

U32 fired her torpedo. Like one of the first shots at the *Empress* it exploded prematurely about 50 yards from its target. *Balzac* saw no aggressor, but even so mistook the explosion for shellfire and took off at top speed away from it, at this point sending out a distress signal.

Balzac's top speed was not great, perhaps about 11 knots, but it was certainly too much for the U-boat. *U32* was left behind and did not get another shot at that time. But during the day *Balzac* not catching up with the convoy, assumed a zig-zag pattern for safety's sake and by so doing virtually lessened the lineal distance she could cover. The U-boat was sailing on a direct course and in the evening she caught up with *Balzac*. The time was 1822. And *Harvester* was there.

When Jenisch rose to periscope depth and upped his periscope to observe his victim, he must have committed the cardinal error of not scanning the horizon. Had he done so he could not have missed seeing *Harvester*. The first he did see of her was when she was bearing down on him to ram.

Jenisch crash-dived (a term which, whilst quite explicit, is nevertheless incorrect, or so the author is informed by an ex-RN submarine commander of his acquaintance). He felt the pulsations of the fast-moving destroyer's engines above him, knew that depth charges would come and steered away towards *Balzac*, getting as close as he could in the hope that the proximity of the freighter would inhibit the destroyer's attack. Shortly he heard and felt what he thought were five depth charges, and whilst they did not damage his vessel they did, as Thornton had hoped they would, upset the nerves of his crew.

Jenisch turned away from *Harvester* at high speed. After a while he came up again to periscope depth and took another look. He was horrified to find that he was now facing not one but two destroyers, both of which seemed to know where he was and what he was doing.

To remain on the surface was to invite ramming by the two much faster vessels. At sea level he could not escape them. His only hope was to submerge as deep as he could go. He went down to 400 feet, but could still hear the pulsations of ship's engines above him. He waited nervously for the concussions of the depth charges he knew had to come. There was a weird tap-tap-tap on the hull which he identified as asdic transmissions. And then the horrifying concussions burst out all around him, tossing his vessel about helplessly, seeming to go on for ever. His crew were terrified and for some moments were rendered almost mindless.

It was Dallmeyer's 14.

All electrical equipment stopped working. This in itself was calamitous enough, but seconds later when the lights went out it was sheer disaster. They were in the blackest of black darkness. Air pressure was leaking, some of it into the hull, making breathing uncomfortable. Jenisch went aft using a hand torch to see what damage had been done. *It was a disaster*! In addition to the aforementioned damage he now found that his ballast tanks on both sides were crushed in. Water was coming in astern, and they were a long, long way down. Would Jenisch be able to get them up again? It was at that time a momentous question.

That he *did* get the U-boat to the surface we already know. He 'blew everything'—thus causing the massive bubbles seen by the *Highlander*—and went full ahead on his electric motors using his hydroplanes to guide him upwards, the upward lift increasing as his remaining air expanded.

And then, for some reason he fired two torpedoes. Or someone did. But what on earth for? According to Dallmeyer they were not heading for any target. And if anything the discharge would have inhibited the U-boat's rise to the surface, for water would have flooded the torpedo tubes. Did someone panic or make a mistake? No one knows. Perhaps Jenisch knew, but he is dead.

In any event, *U32* came up at high speed to break the surface with her bows stuck high out of the water at a 30 degree angle. Once on the surface Jenisch immediately set his diesels to work and for some minutes took *U32* forward at a massive nine knots for fear of sliding back.

But at last Jenisch gave the order to abandon ship and her engines were closed down. The seacocks were opened and the crew emerged to escape their sinking vessel. They did this with speed and discipline with the fear of death on their tails.

They had had enough. But as they entered the water, *High-lander* opened up with cannon and machine-gun. Jenisch saw some of his men hit but there was nothing he could do to help them. These men were members of his gun crew who had manned the gun when the vessel surfaced.

Then a rather bizarre incident emerged. Oberleutnant Fritz Wentzel, Second-in-Command, stuttered. When Jenisch ordered 'Abandon Ship', Wentzel was too highly excited to repeat the order to his gunners and whilst he stood there trying to get the words out, they might easily have returned the British gunfire. Had they done so, the Royal Navy would have shown no mercy. There was the loss of the *Empress* still on everyone's mind and the Royal Navy was not thinking in terms of being nice to Germans. It was a tricky moment.

Presumably Wentzel got his order out in time and the gunners abandoned ship—but not before some of them had been shot. The last to leave *U32* was the Engineer, Anton Thimm. It was also he who had opened the seacocks.

* * *

Harvester held the U-boat in the beam of her searchlight. They watched as *U32* slid slowly, stern first, into the depths and with a healthy-sized 'plup and sizzle' and an immense sucking-in disturbance of the sea as the waters closed over her, she disappeared.

Harvester however, was not yet satisfied and prepared to fire a 14 pattern of depth charges. But then they heard shouting from the sea and saw men swimming towards them—sufficient to indicate that there was no deception and that the crew had abandoned. *Harvester* reversed her engines and stopped in the middle of the swimmers and they were hauled aboard. *Harvester* picked up 29, *Highlander* four.

There was, however, still the possibility that *U32*—unknown then to the British by her number—had not been operating alone and that she was part of a pack, the sort of thing which was to cost Britain massive losses in shipping during the next three years. The two destroyers therefore headed back for the convoy, sweeping each side of the *Balzac*.

On board *Highlander*, the senior U-boat officers were immediately interrogated. Jenisch, Wentzel and Thimm were

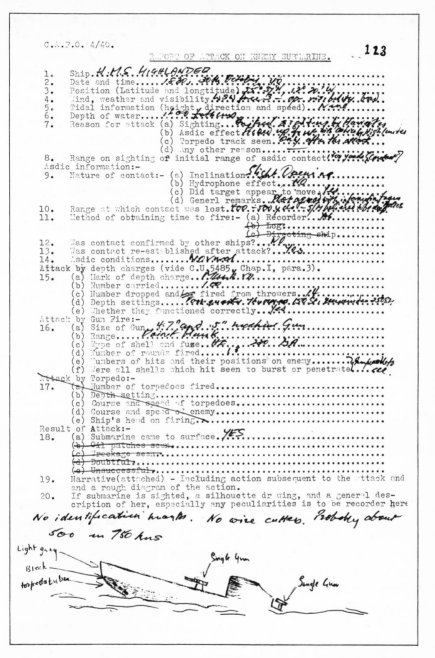

C.A.F.O. 4/40.   123

REPORT OF ATTACK ON ENEMY SUBMARINE.

1. Ship. H.M.S. HIGHLANDER
2. Date and time..... 1830. 30th October 1940
3. Position (Latitude and longitude) 55.54 N, 12.10 W
4. Wind, weather and visibility. W24 force 3 — op. visibility bad
5. Tidal information (height, direction and speed). None
6. Depth of water.... 1100 fathoms
7. Reason for attack (a) Sighting. Ships sighting by Havister
                       (b) Asdic effect. Obtained up to time on Asdic, slight cavitation
                       (c) Torpedo track seen. Only after the attack
                       (d) any other reason....
8. Range on sighting or initial range of asdic contact. 400 yds contact?
    Asdic information:-
9. Nature of contact:- (a) Inclination. Slight Opening
                        (b) Hydrophone effect. No
                        (c) Did target appear to move. No
                        (d) General remarks. Not opened up
10. Range at which contact was lost. 400 - 500 yds
11. Method of obtaining time to fire:- (a) Recorder. No
                                       (b) Log.
                                       (c) Directing ship.
12. Was contact confirmed by other ships? No
13. Was contact re-established after attack? Yes
14. Asdic conditions. Normal
    Attack by depth charges (vide C.U. 5485, Chap.I, para.3).
15. (a) Mark of depth charge. Mark IV
    (b) Number carried. 100
    (c) Number dropped and/or fired from throwers. 14
    (d) Depth settings. Ten events. Averages 150 St remainder 250 St
    (e) Whether they functioned correctly. Yes
    Attack by Gun Fire:-
16. (a) Size of Gun. 4.7" and .5" machine Gun
    (b) Range. Point blank
    (c) Type of shell and fuse. HE. 1-1 ... 200. DA
    (d) Number of rounds fired....
    (e) Numbers of hits and their positions on enemy....
    (f) Were all shells which hit seen to burst or penetrate.... see
    Attack by Torpedo:-
17. (a) Number of torpedoes fired....
    (b) Depth setting....
    (c) Course and speed of torpedoes....
    (d) Course and speed of enemy....
    (e) Ship's head on firing....
    Result of Attack:-
18. (a) Submarine came to surface. YES
    (b) Oil patches seen....
    (c) Wreckage seen....
    (d) Doubtful....
    (e) Unsuccessful....
19. Narrative(attached) - Including action subsequent to the attack and
    and a rough diagram of the action.
20. If submarine is sighted, a silhouette drawing, and a general des-
    cription of her, especially any peculiarities is to be recorded here

No identification marks. No wire cutters. Probably about
500 in 750 tons

Light grey
Black
torpedo tubes

Single gun

Single Gun

*HMS Highlander's report on the action against U32 with a sketch of the
crippled U-boat surfacing, showing its torpedo tubes. (PRO, Kew, and
Controller of HM Stationery Office; a copy of the original document
ADM 199/121, p113)*

the only members of the crew experienced in submarine warfare, the others being new arrivals on the scene with no previous experience in action. From the questioning, Dallmeyer concluded that *U32* had, in fact, been operating alone and therefore, at Jenisch's request and after some hesitation, he agreed to return to the scene of the action and by amazing good luck found four more survivors—men who most certainly would have died within a few hours in the icy cold wintry sea. Of the complement of 43 men, 37 survived. Six died either of gunshot wounds or by drowning.

The story of the *Empress of Britain* was concluded.

Appendix 1

How many bombs?
How many attacks?
How many hits?

On a battlefield the number of bombs dropped is irrelevant except in regard to the damage they do to the enemy. On the same basis—damage to the enemy—a strike by a single 550 lb bomb on a single ship is a massive factor. Two strikes by two 550 lb bombs are devastating. Three or four of them and the result is horrific. And on that basis the situation on the *Empress of Britain* may be described as horrendous.

The victims were confronted with fear and confusion, with riotous, ten-feet high flames and huge volumes of the blackest of black smoke. For many hours they lived with the fear of being blown sky high at any moment. There were no lights and there was no water. Communication with any part of the ship other than the part they were in was impossible. For most of these terrifying hours they had no means of escaping the fires.

There were 643 victims of Jope's bombs, many of them killed and injured. There was a Captain distraught with worry, not only about the victims, of which he was one, but about the destruction of one of the world's most important merchant ships of which he personally was in charge. It is therefore understandable when persons, like Dr Delorme, said they were not counting bombs. Nevertheless, in view of the terrifying situation which only a couple of bombs could cause, it may be worthwhile trying to find out how many there really were.

Differing opinions were expressed by a number of people who gave evidence at the Board of Enquiry on November 1940 at St Enoch hotel in Glasgow. In the following extracts, the italics are the author's.

Captain Charles Sapsworth

Question 43.   About how many bombs were dropped?
Answer.   I should think about *five direct hits and I saw one miss* in the water.
Question 44.   How many machine-gun attacks were there?
Answer.   There were *two distinct attacks* on the bridge but I did not see any others. [In his report he said, 'The plane made *two attacks* from aft and then changed his tactics and made *two or three attacks* from forward. At the first attack *a large incendiary bomb* penetrated to the main lounge'.

Able Seaman Henry Petch, Royal Navy

Question 279.   How many bombs did you see dropped?
Answer.   *Three*, Sir.
                 [Seaman Petch saw *two hits*.]

Able Seaman John Webb, Royal Navy

Question 347.   Did you see the first bomb dropped?
Answer.   Yes, Sir.
Question 348.   Where was it?
Answer.   On the tennis court, port side.
Question 349.   Did you see any other bombs dropped?
Answer.   I thought there were *two* in the first attack and then he made more attacks. The second time he dropped *two* bombs which missed. At the third attack *a bomb* dropped just forward of the 3-inch gun on the starboard side.

Chief Steward Lawrence Moss

Question 528.   What happened in the dining room when you heard the whistle?
Answer.   I was just leaving my room.
Question 529.   What did you do then?
Answer.   I heard *another bomb* fall very quickly afterwards.
Question 540.   When you came out of your room did you feel any blast or concussion?

Answer.   I felt a *terrible thump*, the ship shook, then immediately afterwards *another one*.

Major George Trotter

Question 134.   Will you tell us where you were when the first bomb exploded?

Answer.   I was walking on the sports deck with Colonel Lord Yarborough ... The next moment *a bomb* hit the boat deck about 15 to 20 yards in front of us. It went straight through ... I got up and ran back towards the entrance to the sun deck cabins. We found these had already been hit by a *bomb* which must have fallen at the same time, as I only heard one explosion ... I could not get back to the main part of the ship because of the fire and smoke ... Then there was *a very heavy explosion* which appeared to be further aft. [Later Major Trotter heard many explosions which he at first thought were bombs but later realised were 6-inch ammunition (or fuses) exploding.]

Captain Harold Turner, (Ship's Adjutant)

Question 193.   Will you say briefly what you did?

Answer.   When the *first* bomb dropped I flung myself down to the deck. That explosion was quickly followed by *another one*.

Lieutenant Commander Charles Garrett, Royal Navy

Question 168.   What sort of bomb do you think the first was?

Answer.   High explosive.

Question 169.   What do you think caused the fire to spread so quickly?

Answer.   Woodwork and varnish.
                 [Commander Garrett's personal report to the Board of Enquiry says, '... My gun crew opened fire almost simultaneously with the *first* bomb ... I left D deck, ran up the main staircase and found a fire raging on the lounge deck. The lights had gone out. There were *several further explosions* about this time ...]

Petty Officer George Adlam, Royal Navy

Question 234.   Did you hear the HA gun fire?

Answer.   I can't be certain as there were *so many*
                 explosions going on.

Captain Bertram Nicholson, Royal Navy
Question 116.   . . . Was that the air raid alarm?
Answer.   Yes, the air raid alarm. The air raid alarm, *the*
                 bomb explosion and our own machine-gun
                 fire all went off together. By the time I arrived
                 on the bridge *the bomb* had exploded . . . As I
                 turned to go back to the bridge, I heard *one or*
                 two more explosions but I am not certain if
                 they hit the ship . . . A few minutes afterwards
                 I saw the enemy bomber coming down from
                 ahead . . . When he dropped *his bomb* I saw it
                 clearly all the time.

The Findings of the Board of Enquiry said:
Para 5   'The evidence shows that it is probable that
                 the plane released two bombs during the first
                 attack, one hit abreast the centre funnel,
                 started a serious fire in the Mayfair Lounge,
                 the other dropping somewhere in the vicinity,
                 probably slightly abaft it . . .'
Para 6   '. . . carried out another attack from astern,
                 again dropping two bombs, one of which
                 missed the stern, the other hitting the stern,
                 failing to explode and rolling over the side. A
                 third and final attack with bombs was made
                 scoring a hit near the 3-inch gun position,
                 putting the gun out of action and starting a
                 serious fire . . . which subsequently caused the
                 6-inch gun ammunition to explode . . . There
                 is reason to believe that a second bomb of this
                 attack hit the sun deck causing more damage
                 and fire.'

Summing up, we have something like this:

	Hits (incendiary)	Attacks	Bombs dropped	Hits (high explosive)	Misses
Sapsworth	1	5	6	4	1
Petch		3	3	2	1
Hipwell		3	3	2	1
Webb		3	5	3	2
Moss			2	2	
Trotter		3	3	3	
Turner			2	2	
Garrett		Several	Several	Several	
Adlam			Several	Several	
Nicholson		3	4	2	2
Board Findings		3	6	4	2

What did the man who released the bombs, Oberleutnant Bernard Jope, have to say? In view of what happened on the *Empress*, his answer is surprising. The following is a quoted extract from a letter from Bernard Jope dated 22 September 1982 (author's italics):

> 'My air gunner fired during the attack from the lower arms stand from his 2 cms cannon and we were already being attacked at our first attack, by the ship with tracers. (My target aim in front of the cockpit window was destroyed!) I had *4 250 kg–SC bombs* on board and dropped *one* at our first attack and this one hit. I turned, repeated the attack a second time, again from aft, again only *one bomb*—this was a miss. I decided to drop the remaining *2 bombs* at the third attack, this time from the front. From these two, only *one* hit the target, so that Empress now had *two direct hits*. Certainly we were pleased about the success.'

Three attacks—not five as stated by the Captain; *four* bombs—not six as stated by the Captain and the Board; *two* hits—not four as stated by the Captain and the Board; and *no* incendiaries, as the Captain, quite reasonably, stated.

In a further letter dated 9 November 1982, Bernard Jope says:

> 'Concerning the hits on the ship—we had only two—one on the first attack and one on the third attack. The second attack failed. We dropped four bombs, each 250 kgs. We had no incendiaries on board.'

Bernard Jope is probably right, and to support him we have the following from Jane's *All the World's Aircraft* (author's italics):

'. . . the six remaining C-O Condors were fitted with three 7.92 mm MG15 machine-guns and *racks for four 250 kgs bombs* and by the summer of 1940 I/KG 40 [A German Air Group] had begun a campaign that was to make the Condor, in Churchill's words, "The scourge of the Atlantic" One of its first victims was the "Empress of Britain" . . .'

But there are other factors. One is simply an off-the-cuff remark by Dr Delorme who said, 'In regard to the number of hits on the ship . . . there were certainly more than two. The German pilot is too modest.'

The last factor is contained in the British Intelligence translation of a message sent to German High Command in Berlin from Bordeaux-Merignac. It says (author's italics):

'. . . Attack at 1030 on SS Empress of Britain (42,000t) in square 1676/25 West, course east *with 6 SC 250*, 2 SC in target.'

In other words, although the claim to have scored only two hits remain, Jope—unless the translation or transmission was in error—did have *six* 250 kg bombs on board and not just four. Did Jope miss four times out of six? Or did he after the event underclaim on the number of hits? The immediate devastation seems to show that he did.

Appendix 2

Did Bernard Jope signal and deceive?

There were several reports by gunners and lookouts that before attacking, the approaching aircraft signalled. The evidence seems pretty firm, as given in the following extracts from the Board of Enquiry Proceedings (author's italics):

Petty Officer Arthur Cluett, RN (Lookout on Upper Bridge)
Question 208. What did it do then?
Answer. Carried on circling to the starboard quarter, and then fired what appeared to be *one green and one white Very light.*
Question 209. What did you take that to mean?
Answer. As their challenge to us.
Question 210. What did it do then?
Answer. Circled straight over the midship part of the ship and opened fire with machine-guns.

Leading Signalman Sidney Newstead, RN (Leading Signalman of the Watch on Upper Bridge)
Question 244. Did you see it fire any Very lights or signals?
Answer. Yes, Sir.
Question 245. What colour were they?
Answer. I am not sure if it was *a green and a white* or *two green.*

Able Seaman Henry Petch, RN (Trainer, 3-inch HA gun)
Question 278. Will you say what happened when you first saw the aircraft?

Answer.   I watched the aircraft approaching down the
                 port side at long range towards the stern (about
                 3,000 yards off). *He flashed a lamp from his*
                 cabin once only and we were dubious as to
                 whether it was friendly or enemy. Then he
                 turned towards the stern and it was seen that
                 he had four engines, which told us definitely
                 it was enemy. He then came towards the stern
                 of the ship, *dropping two red Very lights.*

All three witnesses seem to be pretty well convinced about the
signals and, although Newstead did not say at what point in
the attack they occurred, both Cluett and Petch say the same
thing—as the plane was coming towards the stern of the ship.

Why would Jope have signalled? There could have been two
reasons. The first that he was not at first sure that the vessel was
an enemy. It might have been a German or French ship trying to
make its way to a German or French port. The *Bremen* did
successfully make such a journey. Plans made by the High
Command to bring back an important merchant vessel would
probably not have been disclosed to a reconnaissance plane for
the sake of security, unless it were definitely assigned to the task
of escorting such a ship through dangerous waters.

The only other reason would have been to deceive the ship
into a false sense of security by pretending to be friendly.
Related to the times there was nothing wrong with that, for
deception is both a major tactic and a major strategy in war.
But if this happened why does Jope not say so? After all these
years no one is going to be upset about it. But this is what Jope
does say (author's italics):

> 'For answering your last questions—we on the attack to the
> Empress never flashed any signals, neither green or red, nor
> white nor any other colour! *Only our position lights were*
> *set—steady green on the right side and red on the left side—*
> and no flash lights, like today on modern planes. (Anti-
> collision lights!)'

The author detects a note of asperity in Bernard Jope's letter as
though he were offended or embarrassed at the suggestion that
he had signalled and deceived. Still, the lookouts certainly did
see something. Maybe it *was* the position lights. But why on

earth would position lights be switched on during a dangerous mission in wartime, in an area which almost certainly was under enemy surveillance? And what is stranger still, when his plane was more than 900 miles from its base?

Appendix 3

'Highly commendable . . .'

As far as can be ascertained, the only awards made as a result of the action surrounding the attack upon the *Empress of Britain* were three 'Mentioned in Dispatches'. This is probably reasonable since those concerned were simply subjective victims of attack. But since some awards were made it is reasonable to ask whether all whose actions deserved an award were given one. A 'Mention' went to each of the following:

Third Officer Allen Morison
Fifth Officer George Bonwick
Chief Steward Lawrence Moss.

The Findings of the Board stated that the actions of these three officers were highly commendable. Fair enough. But Dr Delorme got nothing. In the whole of the Proceedings and Findings his name does not even arise except in Able Seaman Webb's evidence where he mentioned the ship's doctor was in the same boat as he was, and when Bonwick stated that he called over from one lifeboat to another to get the assistance of the doctor. This is really remarkable, because the indisputable fact is that he did a great deal of very fine and dedicated work on the *Empress*, in the lifeboats and later on board *Echo*. When he was asked if he had been granted any award he answered quite simply, 'None—and to my mind quite rightly'.

Lieutenant-Commander Garrett was a little luckier than Delorme. But not much. The Findings state that '. . . we find the behaviour and action taken by the Naval Contingent under the charge of Lieutenant-Commander C. R. Garrett was beyond criticism . . .'

And that, as it might be put, was his lot.

But let us refer back to the report presented to the Enquiry by the Naval Stores Officer, Mr F. Willis, given on page 149, for corroboration of the excellent behaviour and fine work done by Garrett. There can be no doubt that he acted with great resolution, courage and responsibility. The fact that he failed to express himself adequately either in his verbal evidence at the Board of Enquiry or in his written report should not really detract from the worthiness of the efforts he made.

Reviewing the actions of the persons involved, one is tempted to wonder upon what criteria the awards were made. But then the world is full of unknown and unrecognized heroes, and other heroes who perhaps have their heroism thrust upon them.

But then there is CPO Ransome who, with Garrett and others, struggled through smoke and flame at the risk of his life to get to a boat to save stranded passengers. And Ransome again, who risked his life in swimming a mile or so in the open sea to try to retrieve one of the lifeboats which lesser men than he had allowed to float away empty. And Able Seaman Giles who went with him. And what about the selfless and purposeful courage and mateship of Petch and company? And what about poor Jimmy England?

All these men, with the exception of Delorme, Giles and England, gave evidence at the Enquiry in the same way as Bonwick, Morison and Moss. Perhaps they did not say enough. Perhaps they were not asked the right questions. Perhaps there was not enough 'I' in what they said. Or perhaps, as in Garrett's case, there was too much 'I'! And perhaps again the members of the Board just did not make any decisions other than the ones which were expedient, or the ones they were expected to make.

Appendix 4

Elevations and deck plans of *Empress of Britain*

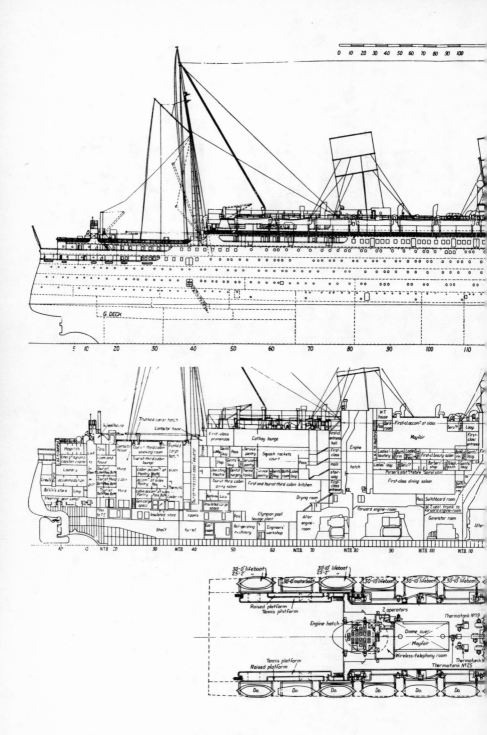

Profile / Deck plan (ship's longitudinal plan)

Scale bar (top): 0 10 20 30 40 50 60 70 80 90 100

Upper profile numbering: 5 10 20 30 40 50 60 70 80 90 100 110

G. DECK

Middle section labels:

Wheelhouse · Trunked cargo hatch · Contactor house · Contactor house · Trunked cargo hatch

First-class promenade · Cathay lounge · W.T. house · First-cl. accom'n at sides · Scru' · Lav.

Hospital · Pass · Tourist-third cabin smoking room · Vents lav. · Pass · Service pantry · Squash rackets court · First-cl hall · First class · Engine · Mayfair · First-cl. accom'n at sides

Lines of squash · capstan engine · room and house · Tourist-third cabin lounge · Shop · Gents' lav. · Service pantry · First class · main · First-cl beauty salon · First-cl. lavatory · Ladies' rm Ladies' lav. · First-cl. lavatory

Laundry · Tourist third accommodation · gear · cabin accom'n at sides · Pantry Bath · Breakfast theatre · Dental surgery · Dental infirmary · Gents' lav. · Ladies' pantry · Gents' lav. · Ladies' lav. · star-way · Barbers' shop · Scru't · Purser's staf'store · store · Spiral stair · Teleph. exch. · Gents' lav.

Crew's · Tourist third · Pantry Bath Wom · Tourist third · First class entrance · First-class dining saloon

Bo'sn's store · Lav. · cabin accom'n at sides · Pantry Pass Bath Cooler rm · Thermotk. · Drying room · Pass · Switchboard room

Steering-gear comp't · gear · Gen cargo space · Pass · Forward engine-room · W.T. cent. trunk to forward engine-room · Generator room

Pass H.T.S. · Insulated cargo space · rooms · Pass · After engine-room

Shaft · tunnel · Insulated store · Ref'rigerating machinery · Olympian pool · Sewage plant · Engineers' workshop · After engine-room · After

Exit room

Lower numbering: A 10 W.T.B. 20 30 W.T.B. 40 50 60 W.T.B. 70 W.T.B. 80 90 W.T.B. 100 W.T.B.

Bottom deck plan labels:

30-0 lifeboat 25-2" · 30-10 lifeboat 25-2" · 30-0 motorboat · 30-10 lifeboat · 30-10 lifeboat · 30-10 lifeboat

Raised platform · Tennis platform · 2 operators · Thermotank Nº19

Engine hatch · Dome over · Mayfair

Tennis platform · Wireless-telephony room · Thermotank Nº...

Raised platform · Thermotank Nº25

Do. · Do. · Do. · Do. · Do. · Do.

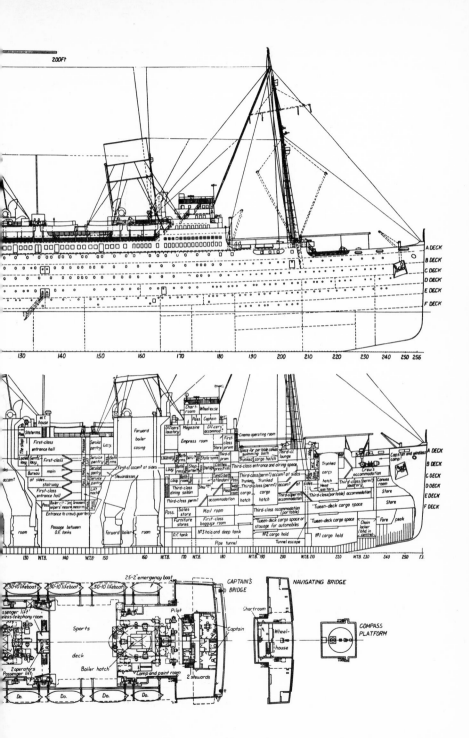

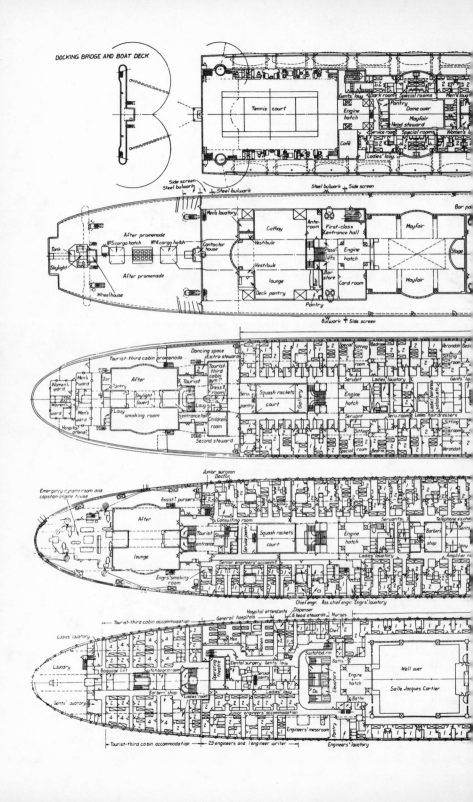

DOCKING BRIDGE AND BOAT DECK

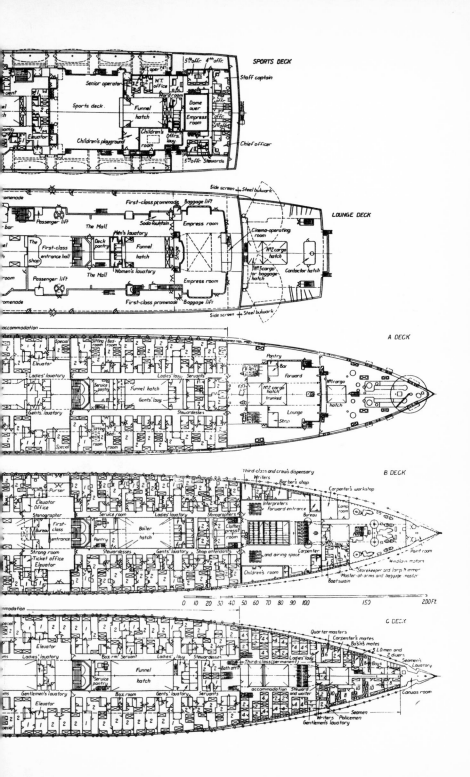

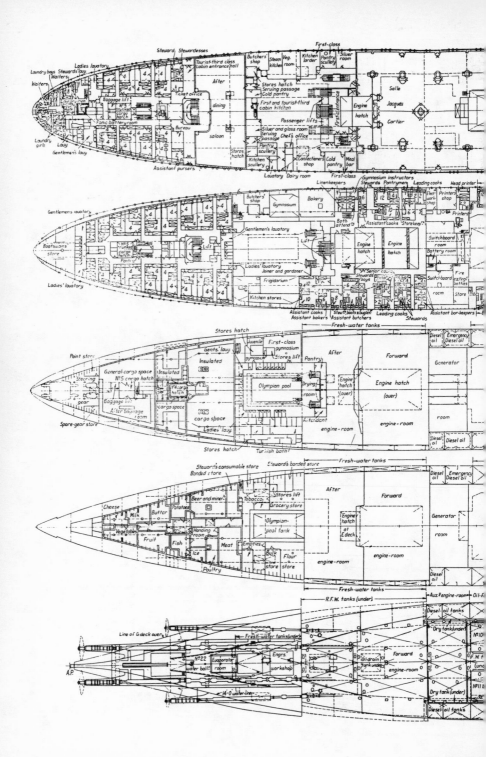

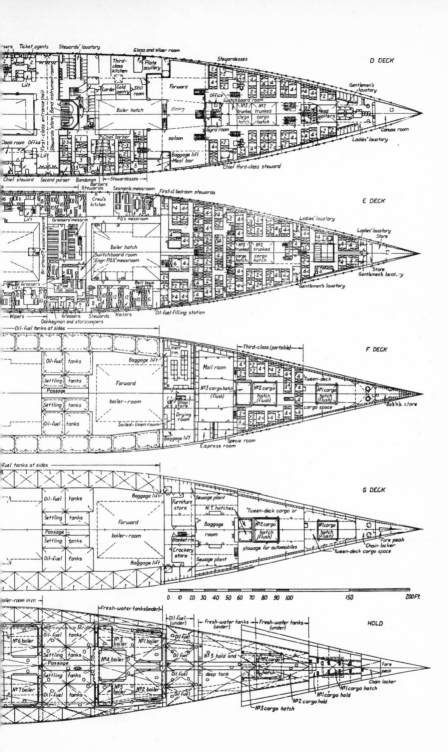

Index